HERITAGE UNL[...]

Guide to free sites in the East of England

D1512880

Hadleigh Castle, Essex

CONTENTS

As well as its many nationally renowned attractions, like Framlingham Castle and Audley End House and Gardens, the east of England is home to a wealth of English Heritage sites to which entry is free. This latest in a series of guidebooks provides a concise but informative introduction to each of these sites, in Bedfordshire, Cambridgeshire, Essex, Hertfordshire, Norfolk and Suffolk. The sites are truly varied, from earthworks and structures of the first centuries AD to the remains of some of the country's most prestigious religious foundations.

The Romans founded their first capital – Camulodunum – at Colchester, while Verulamium, now St Albans, became Roman Britain's third largest town and still boasts a wealth of Roman remains. After the Norman Conquest some of William's closest supporters had extensive estates in the region. They founded religious houses and built themselves fortified dwellings, as the Warenne family did at Castle Acre, that remain dramatic statements of prestige to this day. The region's religious and secular heritage reflects the fortunes of some of the most powerful dynasties of medieval England. Many sites are rare architectural treasures: witness one of Robert Adam's few forays into church building at Mistley, or the inspired early use of classical features that made Old Gorhambury House a showpiece of its time.

Throughout the book, special features highlight particular aspects of the region: its characteristic windmills, for example, and some of the writers and artists who have been inspired by its landscapes. This guide aims to encourage visitors to explore, understand and enjoy some of the lesser-known but no less intriguing monuments in English Heritage's care. The sites are described in alphabetical order within each county. For those who want to see more, a brief guide to English Heritage's paying sites in the region is given at the end of the book.

Near Thetford, Norfolk

WITHDRAWN

East Anglia's long coastline, with its beaches backed by low cliffs or dunes, is both a ready landing ground and a difficult one to defend. Add to this its proximity to mainland Europe, ease of access to London and several sheltered anchorages, and it seems like an open invitation to invade. The Romans found the coast vulnerable to attack as early as the second century AD. They constructed four 'Saxon Shore forts' in the region, part of a series of nine or more between the Wash and the Solent. Like the others, Burgh Castle in Norfolk stood at the mouth of a major estuary to protect shipping using the port and to house a mobile garrison to patrol the coast. Medieval defences were not so systematic but were impressive nonetheless. Important works include Henry II's Orford Castle, an expensive construction at the mouth of the

Tilbury Fort, Essex

River Ore designed in part to increase the kings's control and influence in East Anglia. Fifty years later, Henry III ordered sizeable defensive walls round Yarmouth, which are amongst the best preserved in Britain.

Henry VIII devised the first true system of coastal defences from 1538, when invasion from France and the Holy Roman Empire seemed inevitable. Royal Commissioners identified King's Lynn, Weybourne, Yarmouth, Lowestoft, Aldeburgh, Orford, the Orwell (Landguard and Harwich) and Tilbury as most in need of bulwarks – artillery fortifications – to deny an enemy fleet access to anchorages from which they could land troops at leisure.

Extract from the 1588 Weybourne fortifications showing Norfolk coastal defences

THE COASTAL DEFENCES OF EAST ANGLIA

These locations continued to influence the siting and construction of coastal defences for the next 400 years. At many sites existing defences were replaced or progressively updated. Usually this was in response to improvements in weaponry or some urgent threat of invasion, or both. During periods of peace, defences were often left with minimal resources and reduced garrisons, but with each invasion fear these same sites were strengthened or rebuilt to withstand the latest forms of artillery. So it was with activity caused by the Spanish Armada of 1588; the Dutch Wars between 1652 and 1678; the Napoleonic Wars of 1793–1815; the impact of the steam-powered ironclad warship and the rifled gun between 1840 and 1860; and the growth of German military and naval power between 1880 and 1900. Invasion fears during the two world wars caused the rapid building of coastal fortifications, and even the Cold War saw new constructions connected with national defence at Orfordness and elsewhere.

Tilbury and Landguard in particular illustrate how forts were progressively modified to house ever more powerful guns. Just as important – though never put to the test – were the hundreds of smaller structures, such as the string of Napoleonic War Martello Towers above the Suffolk and Essex beaches, and the defensive GHQ (General Head-quarters) line of pillboxes constructed during the Second World War from Canvey Island to Yorkshire. Not until 1956 was the coastal artillery defence system finally declared redundant.

Today there are abundant remains of the defences that have guarded our shores for over 500 years. From large forts to tiny pillboxes, many are striking and dramatic structures; important and fascinating monuments of our national heritage and witness to the evolving demands of national security.

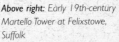

Above right: Early 19th-century Martello Tower at Felixstowe, Suffolk
Right: WW2 'Type24' pillbox at Weybourne Hope, Norfolk

BEDFORDSHIRE, CAMBRIDGESHIRE, ESSEX & HERTFORDSHIRE

The development of these western counties of the east of England differed from that of Norfolk and Suffolk, which were more isolated historically and were influenced to a great extent by trade opportunities across the North Sea. In contrast, Essex and Hertfordshire responded to their proximity to the capital, while Bedfordshire and Cambridgeshire looked west towards the agricultural and industrial patterns of the Midlands.

By the 1st century BC Colchester in Essex was the capital of the Catuvellauni tribe under Cunobelin – Shakespeare's Cymbeline.

Left: Houghton House, Bedfordshire

Opposite: Wood Walton Fen, Cambridgeshire

He defended his capital with substantial earthworks that are still visible in places around the town, for example at Lexden and Bluebottle Grove. The Romans were sufficiently impressed to select Colchester as their capital, Camulodunum, in 43 AD, but seventeen years later Boudicca led the Iceni south from the Fens and laid waste to the town. She then unleashed her wrath on Verulamium – modern St Albans – but the Romans quickly rebuilt and stretches of their city walls and gates remain.

Further north, Cambridgeshire, aside from its internationally renowned university, remains dominated by the Fens; a landscape also characterised by numerous medieval churches, like Isleham, that were built along the 'shore' at the Fen edges. These once marshy wastes were the base for an English rebellion against the Normans led by Hereward the Wake, whose story was

told by Victorian novelist and Cambridge graduate Charles Kingsley. The Normans built castles across the region, like Berkhamsted in Hertfordshire, to defend their new territory.

The wild Fens that Hereward knew were not tamed until the 17th century, when drainage engineers transformed them into rich alluvial farmland. Further west, Bedfordshire was more closely allied agriculturally to the open-field system characteristic of the Midlands. In contrast, Essex and its Hertfordshire and Suffolk borders were a mix of sunken lanes and patchwork fields – the landscapes so lovingly depicted by Constable in the 18th century. But the importance of agriculture to the area is far older, attested by the scale and craftsmanship of farm buildings like 15th-century Prior's Hall Barn in Essex.

Despite their differences, the counties are bound to historical East Anglia by a common geology and lack of good building stone. The Romans' brick- and concrete-making technology did not outlast them; instead, flint and timber were the norm, roofed with the thatch that was freely available from the Fens. Fine limestone dressings were restricted to the richest homes and churches. The region's clay deposits, and necessity, made it the first part of the country to redevelop brick making as an industry, from the 13th century. Brick was used to great effect in beautiful country homes like Houghton House, built by 17th-century poet and socialite Mary, Dowager Countess of Pembroke, and Bedfordshire's brickworks have long been a mainstay of the area's economy.

View into the nave of St Botolph's Priory, Essex

● Longthorpe Tower

CAMBRIDGESHIRE

Isleham Priory Church

Denny Abbey and ●
Farmland Museum

Bushmead
Priory ●

Duxford Chapel

BEDFORDSHIRE

Houghton House

● *Wrest Park Gardens*

● *Audley End House*

Mistley Towers

De Grey
Mausoleum,
Flitton

Prior's Hall Barn,
Widdington

St Botolph's Priory

Lexden Earthworks &
Bluebottle Grove,
Colchester

St John's
Abbey Gate

HERTFORDSHIRE

ESSEX

Old Gorhambury House
Roman Wall, St Albans

Berkhamsted
Castle

Waltham Abbey
Gatehouse & Bridge

● *Hill Hall*

Hadleigh Castle

Tilbury Fort
●

9

DE GREY MAUSOLEUM, FLITTON

History

The de Grey family are well known for creating the beautiful formal gardens at Wrest Park, Silsoe, in the early 18th century. Their mausoleum is attached to the mid-15th-century parish church of St John at nearby Flitton and contains a remarkable collection of monuments spanning nearly three centuries. The structure was originally a chapel added to the church at the beginning of the 17th century by Henry, sixth Earl of Kent, to receive his own monument. His work was much altered when the mausoleum was enlarged in 1704 by Henry de Grey, the twelfth earl and subsequently first Duke of Kent, to create a cruciform structure attached to the north and east arms of the chancel. The building has prominent Dutch gables and, unusually for a mausoleum, is well lit with large east-facing windows. Its external design, though striking, was apparently intended to remain appropriate to the character of the church, with castellated parapets and Gothic

detailing in the windows. It is likely that the southern limb of the mausoleum was substantially altered in the 19th century to accommodate the monuments of Thomas, second Earl de Grey, and his family, during which the external walls were rendered and the east window of the southern arm was blocked. The exposed brickwork on the northern limb is a fine example of Flemish bond.

Description

Access to the mausoleum is from inside the church, through an 18th-century wrought-iron screen, and the interior is relatively simple. All four chambers open to the crossing through tall, plain, round-headed arches. The earliest monuments are in the 6th Earl's original western arm of the building, and include a brass to Sir Harry Grey (d 1545) that was moved there when this first part of the mausoleum was built. The tomb of the sixth Earl himself, who died in 1614, is visible from the chancel and

Monumental brass engraving of Sir Harry Grey

is of richly coloured alabaster, with painted effigies of Henry and his wife Mary lying on a large tomb chest. The next substantial monument is to the tenth Earl, who died in 1651, and his wife Amabell who survived him by 47 years. Though similar in form to the sixth Earl's it clearly reflects the classical influences of its time. The central chamber and the north and east arms of the mausoleum contain monuments to Henry, first Duke of

Dutch gables and crenellated parapets of the exterior

Below left: *Detail of the tombs*

Kent, his two wives and his children, all of whom pre-deceased him. The monument to Henry himself shows the Duke in Roman armour. It is attributed to Michael Rysbrack and is considered one of the finest examples of its kind. The final monument in this chamber, to Philip Yorke, second Earl of Hardwicke (d 1790), is of a popular neo-classical design showing a mourning woman beside an urn. Originally in the south chamber, Thomas, the second Earl, moved it here as part of his final alterations to the mausoleum. The south arm now contains the later Victorian monuments, to Thomas (d 1859) and his wife Lady Henrietta (d 1848) and three of their children.

Through Flitton, attached to the church on unclassified road, 1½ miles W of A6 at Silsoe. *OS Map 153, ref TL 059359.* Open weekends only. Keykeeper: Mrs Stimson, Tel 01525 860094

11

Houghton House, showing the classical centrepiece on the west front

Right: *Discretion, Prudence, Piety and Charity welcoming Christian to the Palace Beautiful, from John Bunyan's The Pilgrim's Progress*

is reputed to be the model for the 'Palace Beautiful' in John Bunyan's *The Pilgrim's Progress*, published in 1678.

Houghton would have been the scene for lavish entertaining; the Countess of Pembroke was a major poet and patron of the arts and moved in the highest circles, with James I among her many visitors. When the countess died in 1621 the house reverted to the king who presented it to the Bruce family; Robert Bruce, Earl of Ailesbury, was a key figure in the restoration of Charles II to the throne. Houghton passed to the 4th Duke of Bedford in 1738 and became the home of his eldest son, the Marquis of Tavistock, who died in a hunting accident in 1767. By 1794 the 5th Duke of Bedford, having no further use for Houghton, gutted the house and sold its fittings. Nothing now remains inside the house to hint at its former glory, however, its wooden

History

Built around 1615 for Mary, Dowager Countess of Pembroke, Houghton House is an unusual mix of Jacobean and classical design. It was very likely the work of two architects: John Thorpe, who represented the Jacobean tradition and another, widely thought to have been Inigo Jones who was responsible for introducing the classical style into England. The result was evidently considered a success and Houghton

staircase, thought to have been designed by Sir Christopher Wren, can be seen in the Swan Inn in Bedford. Panelling in the Victoria and Albert Museum may also have come from Houghton.

Thereafter this beautiful house fell into disrepair and during the twentieth century its stonework has continued to deteriorate due to air-born pollution from the brickworks visible on the horizon.

Lithograph of Houghton House by J Hewetson

Description

The house commands spectacular views over the Bedfordshire country-side and would have been a grand setting indeed for the countess' social events. Built in brick with stone facings, its H-plan was very progressive for its time. The centre of the house is two rooms deep and the hall was entered at its midpoint, not close to one end as was the custom. The house has high square towers at each corner and was originally three-storeys high, with a typically busy Jacobean roofline: steeply pitched gables, ornamental chimneys and gilded pinnacles to the towers.

The house's Jacobean features were combined with what was a radical new Italian Renaissance style. On the north and west sides classical centrepieces were introduced, featuring double-storey open loggias with classical columns, round-headed arches and friezes. These features were almost certainly afterthoughts as structurally they are not part of the original concept, and the entrance porch was also a later addition. Owing to the fall of the land to the east there is a high basement underneath, which perhaps remains from an earlier house on the site.

1 mile NE of Ampthill off A421, 8 miles S of Bedford. OS Map 153, ref TL 039395

13

History

Duxford Chapel is an unusual medieval building with an enigmatic history. The old road on which it stands was originally part of the main Royston–Newmarket road, crossing the River Cam at Whittlesford. It has been suggested that a small hamlet had grown by the bridge, centred on the hospital of Whittlesford Bridge. A prior of the hospital is recorded in 1236 as holding one virgate (15 acres) of land in Duxford and it is generally accepted that this is the site of Duxford Chapel; however the distinction, if any, between chapel and hospital is unclear.

There is so far no physical evidence of surrounding buildings or features that might confirm the chapel's use as a hospital, and by 1337 it appears that Duxford had lost any such function and become a 'free chapel' or chantry. When Edward VI dissolved the chantries in 1548 the chapel is said to have been unused for seven years. There may have been an attempt to reinstate it under Queen Mary, as there is a reference to the grant of a pension to the last warden in 1553, but an inventory made just a year later lists the chapel's contents as a single bell, valued at 6s 8d. Thereafter the adjacent 15th-century Red Lion Inn seems to have played a more significant role in local history and evidently prospered while the chapel languished. The latter was used as a barn by the inn and fell into increasing disrepair, and a 19th-century illustration shows it posted with advertisements.

The windows in the south face of the chapel are early 14th century

but the exterior of the east window still has evidence of its elegant tracery. The other windows are early 14th century in style with an unusual cusped design. In one of the windows in the south wall you can see slots for glazing bars and glass, and historic plaster survives on parts of the original walls. The present entrance door and the window immediately to its east replicate the presumed early 14th-century shape.

The east end of the building has the most complete stonework, and the features here clearly indicate that the building was in ecclesiastical use in the 14th century. The arched recess in the north wall is presumed to be an Easter sepulchre, where sacred items were placed during the Easter celebrations. There is a simple rectangular aumbry, or cupboard, on the north corner of the east wall. In the south wall is the piscina, where the priest would have washed his hands and the chalice – you can see the drain in its base – and alongside this his arched seat or sedilia.

Interior of the chapel looking east

Description

The modest flint and cobble chapel retains some attractive medieval features and, despite uncertainties over its origin, the rarity of medieval hospitals lends added interest. The rectangular chapel is simply built, with dressed limestone surrounds to the windows, buttresses and doors. The brick repair to the west wall and much of the inside of the large east window is of unknown date, and the bricks themselves are quite a mixture,

Adjacent to Whittlesford station off A505. OS Map 154, ref TL 485473

15

Isleham Priory Church retains many 12th-century features

History

This small Norman chapel is the best example in the country of a small Benedictine priory church that has remained substantially unaltered. The walls of the original 12th-century building all survive and only the raising of the nave roof – when the chapel was converted to a barn – has altered its overall shape. To the north you can see earthworks relating to the activities of the small priory community that farmed here and the combination of these survivals with an original priory chapel is also extremely rare.

Isleham Priory was probably founded around 1100 by Count Alan of Brittany. Alan later gave the churches at Isleham and Linton to the Benedictine Abbey of St Jacut-sur-Mer in Brittany. As enemy property during the wars with France Isleham had a troubled history. It did not prosper or expand and in 1254 the monks were moved to Linton. In 1440 Isleham was granted to Pembroke College, Cambridge, and either then or after the Reformation the chapel was converted into a barn.

In centre of Isleham, 16 miles NE of Cambridge on B1104.
OS Map 143, ref TL 642743.
Keykeeper:
Mrs Burton,
18 Festival Road,
5 minutes walk from the church

Description

The chalk-rubble chapel has a nave and chancel, with a semi-circular apse at the east end. The curve at the top of the apse walls shows it originally had a vaulted, half-dome roof. Barnack limestone was used for the internal arches and the earlier doorways and windows. The east window and one in the south side of the nave remain unaltered, but the chancel windows and north doors of both nave and chancel were enlarged in the 13th century. The doorway to the village green, in the south wall of the chancel, was inserted after the monks had moved to Linton and the large cart door replaced the original nave door in the 16th or 17th century.

History

The Colchester earthworks at Lexden and Bluebottle Grove are among the few surviving late Iron Age defences in Britain. They defended the west side of pre-Roman Colchester, Camulodunum, which was occupied by the Iron Age Catuvellauni and their leader Cunobelin. This great defensive system is thought to belong to the 1st century AD.

Many pre-Roman graves have been found in the vicinity of Lexden Dyke, the best known of which lies within the ditch itself and is called the Lexden Tumulus. Excavations in 1924 revealed the burial of an Iron Age nobleman – some say Cunobelin himself – surrounded by luxurious objects.

Description

Lexden Earthworks bound the western side of the site and Bluebottle Grove the southern. The outermost rampart, Gryme's Dyke, is today the most impressive. It ran from the River Colne to the Roman River and can be traced for most of its length. South of the London Road it appears first as a hedge and then as a well-defined bank with a substantial ditch on its west side. This dyke is named after the Devil, 'Gryme', to whom Christians attributed many ancient earthworks whose origins were long forgotten. A footpath follows it for more than a mile. The large gravel pit known as King Coel's Kitchen probably marks the point where the Roman roads from Cambridge and London once converged to cross this dyke.

East of Gryme's Dyke are the remnants of an earlier system: the Triple Dyke, west of Lexden; and Lexden Dyke, which extends south to Bluebottle Grove, and continues north of the Colne as Moat Farm Dyke.

Below: Gryme's Dyke

2 miles W of Colchester off A604. Lexden Earthworks are on Lexden Straight Rd. For Bluebottle Grove turn left from Lexden into Heath Rd, left into Church Lane, right into Beech Hill and follow brown signs.
OS Map 168, Lexden ref TL 965246; Bluebottle ref TL 975245

History

Hadleigh Castle is a romantic ruin of great historical and archaeological interest and the only example of its type in the county. In its heyday it was a high-status residence with impressive defences, home to royalty and beneficiary of a major refurbishment project by Edward III. Hubert de Burgh, Earl of Kent, began construction in about 1230. Only nine years later Henry III seized the castle and thereafter it was made the subject of various grants for life, reverting to the king on the death of

The remains of internal structures and one of Edward III's drum towers

each grantee; it was also occasionally granted to the queens of England as part of their dower. Edward III took possession in 1330 and undertook a programme of refortification in 1360–70, both to strengthen the castle and to make it a more fitting royal residence. Much of what remains at Hadleigh is Edward's work.

After this activity, however, royal interest in the castle waned. It was granted to a succession of nobles, including several wives of Henry VIII, but its royal associations finally ended in 1552 when Edward VI sold it to Lord Riche. Riche appears to have immediately plundered the castle for building stone and by the 17th century it had become a ruin: a subject for antiquarian illustrators but no doubt also a significant landmark for sailors. There are also suggestions that the south-east tower was used as an observation point by revenue officers in the 18th and 19th centuries, which perhaps accounts for the concentration of historical graffiti around the seaward-facing upper windows.

Description

The castle occupies the top of a bluff with long views across the Thames Estuary and along the Essex coast. Its large bailey was defended to the south by the fall of the land and on the north, west and east sides by a ditch or ditches, now entirely infilled. The line of the octagonal curtain wall, with massive towers at its angles, can still be followed.

The barbican is Edward III's work, and was approached by a substantial earth ramp. It had a small tower attached and you can see the pit for the turning bridge as well as parts of the slots for the portcullis. Edward's two eastern 'drum' towers are the most striking parts of the castle ruins and provide a clear statement of his intention to increase the castle's defensive and visual impact. The internal features of both survive well, though the north-east one has been undermined by subsidence. Some stretches of the curtain wall are probably part of Hubert's original construction and the remains of the

Engraving of Hadleigh Castle by Samuel and Nathaniel Buck

living quarters tucked against the western wall were built soon after. Also from the 13th century are the three western towers, which are noticeably different in scale and plan from the others along the wall.

The hill on which Hadleigh Castle was built is now well-known for its landslips and over the centuries the castle has suffered greatly from the instability of the underlying London Clay; the many documentary references to its poor construction and repair reflect this. The western curtain wall was rebuilt several times during the 13th century and excavations in the 1970s suggested that the hall had buttresses added soon after it was built.

³/₄ mile S of A13 at Hadleigh.
OS Map 178, ref TQ 810860.
Tel 01760 755161

19

History

Mistley is a building of considerable architectural significance – one of only two churches designed by Robert Adam, carried out for Richard Rigby of Mistley Hall. Rigby's father had made a great deal of money at the time of the South Sea speculation, and Rigby himself attained further wealth and influence when George III made him Paymaster General of the Forces in 1768. At that time the village of Mistley consisted of warehouses, a granary, a large malting office and new quays. There was also a medieval church, only the porch of which survives, and a new church that Rigby's father had built to the north of the village in 1735. When Rigby hatched a scheme to turn Mistley into a fashionable spa this plain, rectangular brick building was not in keeping with his grand plans.

Rigby originally called in Robert Adam to design a saltwater bath by the river, but this plan was never carried out and instead the architect was put to work on the church in around 1776. Adam's scheme was unusual in that it avoided the standard form of 18th-century parish church design, which consisted typically of a rectangle with a western tower or portico (or both) and perhaps an eastern chancel. Instead, by adding towers at the east and west ends and semicircular porticoes on the north and south sides, Adam created a design that was symmetrical along both the long and short axes. This unusual arrangement was possibly influenced by the design of Roman tombs and the result was most unconventional. Mistley would certainly have stood out from other 18th-century churches.

Painted decoration on the ceiling of the eastern tower

One of the towers that adorned Robert Adam's 1776 church

Sadly for Rigby his grand plans for the spa were unsuccessful. The main body of the church was demolished in 1870 when a new and larger church in the then fashionable Gothic Revival style was built nearby. However, the towers were preserved as a seamark, and made symmetrical by adding the columns from the porticoes to the sides formerly attached to the nave. They were then sold to two local families who intended to use them as mausolea, but this did not happen and they fell into disrepair. They were restored in the 1950s by the distinguished local architect Raymond Erith under the auspices of the Georgian Group.

Description

Even in its ruined state Mistley remains an unusual and interesting site. The towers are built in rendered brickwork with decoration in Portland stone. Tuscan porticos project from the outer sides, topped by small lantern domes. The eastern tower was originally the chancel of the church

The towers are all that remain of the church at Mistley

and inside you can still see its painted commandment boards and a painted representation of the Holy Trinity on the ceiling. The western tower is identical internally, though without the painted decoration. The churchyard contains a number of early to mid-18th-century monuments including an obelisk and a large, polished, black granite Egyptian-style mausoleum to the Norman family.

On B1352, 1½ miles E of A137 at Lawford, 9 miles E of Colchester.
OS Map 169, ref TM 116320.
Key available from Mistley Quay Workshops: Tel 01206 393884

History

Prior's Hall Barn is one of the finest surviving medieval barns in the east of England. In an age when timber was plentiful, and a great barn epitomised the prosperity of a landowner, the building provided scope for the craft of the carpenter on a scale otherwise found only in medieval great halls and roofs of churches.

Soon after the Norman Conquest, Widdington was given by William the Conqueror to the abbey of St-Valery-sur-Somme in Picardy. As lands in foreign ownership became an increasing drain on the English economy, Widdington was subsequently confiscated by Edward III and in 1377 given to William of Wykeham, the powerful Bishop of Winchester. Two years later William founded New College, Oxford, and endowed it with Widdington and it is likely that the barn we see today was built for the college. Though there is no documentary evidence for the date of the barn's construction, tree-ring dating showed that timbers were felled in 1417–42 and the barn's stylistic elements are appropriate for this date.

The massive porches of the 15th-century Prior's Hall Barn

Description

The interior of this substantial timber-framed barn is quite breath-taking. Its crown post roof has 71 pairs of upper rafters, with a further eight pairs of rafters of decreasing size in the hipped ends. It is aisled, with eight bays, and has two great porches that allowed carts bearing the harvest to be unloaded under cover inside. The curved bracing and cusped bargeboards on the gable ends are both characteristic 14th-century features. Except for the doors and cladding, the barn is built of oak and originally comprised some 900 separate pieces of unseasoned timber, the product of approximately 400 trees. There was no ironwork in the original construction: the straps and bolts now supporting aisle ties and other members were added much later. Beside each porch is a small door that gave access when the big doors were not being used. At the bottom of each of these is a cat door and in the apex of the gables is an owl hole, both for controlling vermin.

Farming at Widdington was predominantly arable and the main crops stored in the barn were wheat, barley, oats and rye. On dry days the doors could be left open while hand threshing with flails took place just inside, the draught blowing the husks away leaving the grain to be collected.

Today the only major difference from the original construction is the absence of the great timber partition wall that originally separated the eight bays into three and five. In the 18th century a raised floor was constructed at the east end with under-floor ventilation for drying corn. The timber groundsills for the walls and aisles were laid on foundations that were originally of flint and mortar, the remains of which can be seen on each side of the eastern porch. Nearly all the flintwork has since been replaced with 18th-century or later brickwork.

The spectacular interior with its crown post roof

In Widdington, on unclassified road 2 miles SE of Newport, off B1383 near Audley End. *OS Map 167, ref TL 537318.* Open 1 Apr–30 Sept, 10am–6pm Sat–Sun

23

History

Founded between 1093 and 1100, the priory of St Julian and St Botolph was one of the first religious houses in England to adopt Augustinian rule. This initially gave it authority over other houses of that order in the country to correct abuses, inflict punishments and prescribe regulations. Despite these privileges, St Botolph's remained a small foundation and fund-raising must have been hampered by the existence of the more powerful St John's Abbey a few hundred yards to the south. Its relative poverty means construction would have been a slow process, and the details of the west front indicate a completion date of around 1150.

Imposing Norman arches along the north aisle

When St Botolph's was dissolved in 1536 its possessions were granted to Sir Thomas Audley, Lord Chancellor. Part of the church remained in use as a parish church until the seige of Colchester in 1648, when the Royalist town was attacked by General Fairfax. During the seige the church was largely destroyed by cannon fire and has never been repaired. The nave was used for burials during the 18th and 19th centuries and south of the church the cloister was at one stage laid out as a garden.

Description

Even in its ruined state the priory church is an impressive example of early Norman architecture, and the elaborate west front is one of the best surviving examples from this period. It had flanking towers to the north and south, unusually placed outside the nave aisles, and three doorways. The decoration on these – their mouldings and chevron ornament – are carried out in good quality limestone, but the individual stones are small and were evidently used with great economy. Two rows of interlacing Roman brick arches originally ran continuously across the front between the towers. The remains of a large circular window just touching the top of the upper tier, in the middle of the façade, still has chevron ornament around its outer edge. Within this are traces of the rebate for the wooden frame that held the glazing. What remains of the upper levels of the west front indicate this richness of decoration continued all the way to the roof.

The church was built of flint rubble with arches and dressings in brick – the latter mostly reused from Roman buildings at nearby Colchester. Though simple in design the massive piers and arches of the nave are stunning in effect. The circular piers are strengthened by triple courses of brick and the shallow pilasters running up from their capitals mark the division of the bays and the position of the roof tie-beams. The masonry would originally have been plastered over inside and

St Botolph's Priory, Colchester, c 1804–5, by John Sell Cotman

out and probably painted to imitate ashlar blocks; an effect that can be seen on the similar piers at St Albans Abbey. The base of a wall across part of the south aisle shows there was a chapel at this point, but other than that the internal arrangements of the church have been lost. The fragments of a medieval glazed tile pavement in this aisle are probably not in their original position. Much of the north range of the cloister has been uncovered including the remains of its stone bench.

Nr Colchester Town station.
OS Map 168, ref TL 999249.
Tel 01206 282920

25

Monasteries took root early in the relatively well-populated eastern counties. Within 100 years of St Augustine's mission from Rome in 597 AD, communities were already thriving in Ely, Peterborough, Bury St Edmunds and elsewhere. Though Danish invaders plundered and destroyed them in 869 AD, they were refounded a century later, now regulated by the Rule of St Benedict and thus known as Benedictine houses.

The years following the Norman Conquest of 1066 were marked by an influx of energy, money, new ideas and building skills from Europe. By about 1150 all the old abbeys had been rebuilt, often on a vast scale, and in the most up-to-date Norman style. Norwich and Ely (later also Peterborough and St Albans) became cathedrals, while Bury St Edmunds was one of the largest and richest abbeys in the land.

The new European orders of monks, nuns, canons and friars were unusually well represented in the eastern counties. Norman landowners looked to the French Cluniac

order to establish priories at Thetford and Castle Acre. The Cistercians, an austere reforming order prominent in northern England, had only one house, at Sibton in Suffolk. Many houses of 'regular canons' followed a monastic lifestyle though, unlike monks, they were all ordained priests. The Premonstratensians had an abbey at Leiston, the Augustinians had an early house at St Botolph's, Colchester, while the sole priory of the Canons of the

Above: *Reconstruction of the refectory at 14th-century Leiston Abbey, Suffolk*

Below: *The Octagon at Ely Cathedral, Cambridgeshire*

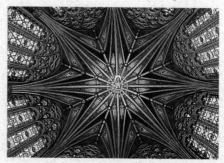

Holy Sepulchre was at Thetford. During the 13th century friaries were established in the region's principal towns – Great Yarmouth had Franciscan, Dominican and Carmelite friaries within its walls. Most towns of any size had one or more monastic communities and many owed their prosperity, or even their very existence, to the presence of the monks.

Medieval pilgrims beat a steady path to the monastic shrines of eastern England. The relics of St Alban, St Etheldreda of Ely and East Anglia's own royal martyr St Edmund at Bury, all drew a stream of pious or penitent pilgrims, both rich and poor. When Thetford Priory was in financial difficulties a series of visions of Our Lady helped replenish the monastic coffers. Walsingham, 'England's Nazareth', became the most frequented pilgrimage centre in the land, visited by almost every king of England. Ironically its last royal visitor was Henry VIII, who walked barefoot and donated a valuable necklace, only to order the destruction of the monastery and shrine a few years later.

The story of the Dissolution of the Monasteries also has an East Anglian twist. In 1536 Thomas Howard, Duke of Norfolk, together with Thomas Cromwell, began seizing monastic property in the north as punishment for rebellion against the suppression of lesser houses already begun by Cromwell. Howard then cleverly tried negotiating surrender closer to home. Castle Acre submitted and its assets were granted to Howard. The process gathered momentum and eventually all monasteries were seized, the last to surrender in 1540 being Waltham Abbey in Essex. Curiously St Benet's in Norfolk slipped through the net and is still technically in existence with the Bishop of Norfolk as its Abbot. The region is rich in monastic remains, a few still in ecclesiastical use while others have been adapted or remain evocative ruins.

Denny Abbey, Cambridgeshire, was established as a cell of Ely Cathedral Priory

History

This elaborate 15th-century gatehouse is all that remains standing of the Benedictine abbey of St John the Baptist that stood outside the walled town of Colchester. The extent of the abbey is still defined by the much-repaired precinct wall, and the gatehouse stands at the centre of the northern boundary.

The abbey was founded in 1095 by Eudo Dapifer, William the Conqueror's High Steward and Constable of Colchester Castle. From its inception the abbey made a major contribution to the development of medieval Colchester and became a wealthy and privileged house, despite losing part of its buildings to fire in 1133. In the late 14th and early 15th centuries, perhaps as a result of the Peasants' Revolt of 1381, the abbey strengthened its defences and the gatehouse was added as part of this revamping around 1400.

St John's was one of a handful of abbeys that refused to surrender to Henry VIII's Commissioners during the Dissolution,

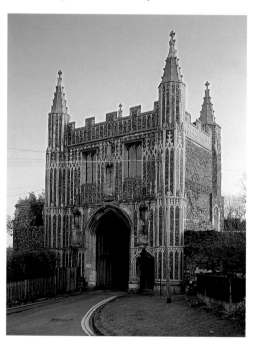

Flintwork panels adorn the elaborate north front of the gate

succumbing only after the execution of the abbot for treason. The property was eventually acquired by the Lucas family who converted some of the abbey buildings into a house. It remained their family seat until the mid-17th century, but as a Royalist stronghold during the siege of Colchester in 1648 it suffered considerable damage. The gatehouse itself was stormed by Parliamentary troops and their artillery destroyed part of the upper storey and damaged the vaulted roof. The site was used to house Dutch prisoners in the 1660s after which the remaining abbey buildings appear to have been demolished; there are no references to occupation after the mid-18th century.

Description

The two-storey gatehouse with its battlemented roof would have made a powerful statement about the strength of the abbey. It has turrets at each corner – higher on the north front – with large pinnacles. The north front is the most richly decorated, with flintwork panels and ornamented niches for statues, and has a pedestrian gate alongside the main carriage entrance.

The gatehouse is principally built of flint and brick with limestone dressings, though Roman and medieval brick has been used at the back of the building. It consists of a gate hall and a porter's lodge. Both carriageway and pedestrian access have ribbed stone vaulting springing from moulded corbels carved with human heads and lions. A doorway in the east wall gives access to the porter's lodge, which is now roofless. A doorway in the west wall once led into a now destroyed adjacent building; a blocked door in the south-west turret once connected this building with the upper room of the gatehouse. The lower part of the structure is mostly original, including the elaborate vaulting. The upper chamber, northern façade and turrets were heavily restored in the mid-19th century, but are believed to be faithful copies of the original work.

S side of central Colchester.
OS Map 168,
ref TL 998248.
Tel 01206 282931

29

Above: 'Harold's Bridge' from the south
Opposite: The gatehouse

In Waltham Abbey off A112.
OS Map 166,
Gatehouse ref TL 381007;
Bridge ref TL 382009.
Tel 01992 702200

History

The gatehouse and bridge at Waltham Abbey are among the remnants of one of the great monastic foundations of the Middle Ages. The abbey is the burial place of King Harold, the last Anglo-Saxon king. His father, Harold Godwin, Earl of Wessex, is said to have been miraculously cured of paralysis by praying before the Holy Rood or Cross at Waltham, and in gratitude refounded the church there in 1030. It was again rebuilt in the early 12th century and the nave of this third building remains in use today. In 1177 the church was refounded as an Augustinian priory,

later an abbey, and became one of the most prosperous and important abbeys in the country. Its fine library was home to the early 13th-century Waltham Bible.

Waltham was the last monastic house in the area to be dissolved and it was granted to the Denny family in 1540. The walls of the post-medieval house that was built on the site can still be seen.

Description

The west and south walls of the late 14th-century abbey gatehouse contain some unusually large red bricks, probably contemporary with the building. In the west wall are two arched gateways, dressed in limestone: a wide carriage entrance and a smaller one for pedestrians. The original bridge to the gatehouse has been replaced, but 'Harold's Bridge' across the Cornmill Stream is 14th century. Of the extensive domestic buildings that lay to the north of the church, only parts of the cloister and chapter house walls are now visible.

BERKHAMSTED CASTLE

History

Set on the northern slope of the small valley of the River Bulbourne, Berkhamsted is a typical motte-and-bailey castle, with a tower or keep built on an earthen mound surrounded by a defensive enclosure. A timber keep was probably built there by William the Conqueror's half brother, Robert, but the oldest stonework dates from the mid-12th

Berkhamsted Castle, its bailey still almost completely surrounded by the curtain wall

century and the ownership of Thomas à Becket while Lord Chancellor. The Pipe Rolls record building work on the site up to 1186.

Despite signing the *Magna Carta* in 1215, King John was so unpopular that the French Prince Louis was invited by rebellious nobles to invade and seize the throne. In December 1216 the castle fell to Louis after a two-week siege, succumbing to a battering from gigantic catapults. By 1254 Berkhamsted was in the possession of King John's second son Richard, Earl of Cornwall, who built a three-storey tower there in that year. The castle eventually became the property of Edward the Black Prince, on his creation as Duke of Cornwall, and it is from this time that its connection with the Duchy of Cornwall dates. During the mid-14th century King John of France was captured by the Black Prince at Poitiers and imprisoned at Berkhamsted.

In the absence of a Prince of Wales, Edward IV gave Berkhamstead to his mother Cicely, Duchess of York.

Thereafter it passed to five queens in succession, ending with Queen Elizabeth I. It is thought, however, that the castle was not occupied after 1495. When Elizabeth I granted a lease of the manor to Sir Edward Carey, in 1580, he built a new house to the west – Berkhamsted Place – which is now almost totally demolished, while the castle itself has gradually fallen into ruin. After the Civil War Berkhamsted was sold, but the sale was annulled at the Restoration in 1660: thereafter the Duchy of Cornwall's ownership has remained unbroken.

Description

Berkhamsted Castle was extremely well defended, with two moats and three sets of earthworks around the oblong bailey, and a further moat around the motte. The substantial motte stands at the north-east corner of the enclosure commanding impressive views over the surrounding countryside, and is a good spot from which to appreciate the castle's

View across the curtain wall to the motte

defences. On the top are the foundations of the circular keep, 18m in diameter, within which is a well.

Though no worked stone remains on the curtain wall, its flint-rubble core survives for almost the full circuit of the bailey. The outer defences also survive well, though they have been disfigured by the railway and road immediately to the south. Access to the site now is from the south-west, but the castle's main entrance was to the south, and would have opened to a wooden bridge across the moat. The remains of some of the structures that occupied the bailey can be seen on the west side, one of which was probably a chapel.

By Berkhamsted station.
OS Map 165, ref SP 995082.
Open all year:
10am–6pm summer;
10am–4pm winter

History

Old Gorhambury House lies just outside St Albans, tucked quietly away in the middle of the private estate of Lord Verulam. Its showpiece is its elaborate entrance porch that was of cutting-edge design in Tudor times. In fact, the standing remains here are just a small part of what was once a very extensive country house. The medieval manor was owned by St Albans Abbey and was home to the Gorham family, but after the Dissolution it was bought by Sir Nicholas Bacon, Lord Keeper of the Great Seal. Sir Nicholas was a prolific builder and spent five years replacing the Gorham's old home with the house whose ruins we see today. When Queen Elizabeth visited in 1572 she is reputed to have remarked, 'My Lord, what a little house have you gotten', to

Sir Nicholas Bacon's showpiece porch

which Bacon smoothly replied, 'Madam, my house is well, but it is you that have made me too great for my house'. Nevertheless, Sir Nicholas built a galleried extension to create a better impression for her second visit in 1577.

Old Gorhambury eventually passed to Sir Nicholas's son Sir Francis Bacon, the celebrated philosopher and Chancellor to James I. Sir Francis further extended the house and created a water garden with a Roman-style banqueting house as its centre-piece. The house was extensively repaired in the 1670s by Sir Harbottle Grimston but by the next century had been allowed to fall into disrepair, and was replaced in 1784 by the present Gorhambury House.

Description

The porch was the focal point of the house: a showy structure on which Sir Nicholas spared no expense. Doric columns flank the entrance arch on the ground floor and Ionic columns and niches flank the upper windows,

The house in 1787, after demolition of the front range

Via entrance to Gorhambury estate and Roman theatre, on A4147. Open all year except 1 June (2-mile walk). Vehicle access limited to 1 May–30 Sept on Thurs pm only: drive to Gorhambury Mansion and walk across the gardens. OS Map 166, ref TL 110076

which originally lit a first-floor room. A Latin inscription records the completion of the house in 1568 and the arms of Queen Elizabeth I appear on the attic storey. The much-weathered wooden statue above was once one of a pair, probably of angels. The porch was constructed from an unusually varied combination of materials, with a brick core faced with local chalk rubble – clunch – and limestone. The dressings were of a higher quality limestone brought from farther afield and some of the more elaborate carvings are in French Caen limestone.

In contrast, most of the rest of the house was built of flint hidden behind pink plaster designed to give the impression of more costly brickwork. A 19th-century plan shows the house was of fairly conventional Tudor design, arranged around a courtyard with the hall opposite the entrance range. It included a chapel and galleried cloister to the west, a ballroom annexe to the east and a further court with the kitchen and offices to the north. All this is rather hard to envisage today as all that remains standing, beyond the porch, are parts of the hall and chapel and the clock tower at the corner of the cloister. Further foundations may survive to some extent in the fields to the east and south of the ruins.

ROMAN WALL, ST ALBANS

History

Once the defensive wall of Roman Verulamium, the city wall of St Albans can still be traced for most of its two-mile circuit. Its towers and gateway foundations give some indication of the importance of Roman Britain's third largest town. The Romans rebuilt the city after Boudicca attacked the first settlement around 60 AD, and by the second century Verulamium had a number of stone public buildings including a theatre and a basilica (town hall), as well as a forum – the open space at the heart of the civic and business quarter. St Albans museum contains a wealth of information about the Roman city

Description

The wall was built between 265 and 270 AD, of mortared flint rubble with layers of brick bonding. It was faced with dressed flints, though very little of this facing survives. Rising from 3m-wide footings, the wall once stood to a height of 5m and was topped by a walkway protected by a 1.8m parapet. Parts of this massive structure still survive up to 4m high, though in places its line is visible only as a change in ground level. At its back was a broad earthen bank up to the level of the walkway and just beyond it a massive defensive ditch, originally up to 29m wide and 6m deep. Sections of this can still be seen.

The foundations of two towers or bastions survive, and east of these are the remains of the impressive London Gate where Watling Street entered the city. This substantial structure had two passageways for vehicles and two for pedestrians, and was defended by flanking towers.

Above: Reconstruction of the London Gate.

Opposite: Mosaic of a horned god from Verulamium.

Below left: Bands of tile were used to strengthen the wall

On S side of St Albans, 1/2 mile from the centre off the A4147. OS Map 166, ref TL 137066

To drive across the Acle Straight from Acle to Great Yarmouth on a clear, bright day is truly a visual treat. As a dozen or more distant windmills gradually come into view there is a sense that England has been left behind and a Dutch landscape painting has been brought to life in its place. Some mills are forlorn, bare shells, while others have freshly-painted white caps or are again in

Above: John Sell Cotman's view of St Benet's Abbey, Norfolk, (1831)

Right: Unusual 18th-century graffiti at St Giles's Church, Totternhoe (Beds), depicts windmills with short square sails characteristic of the late medieval period

full sail. Many 'mills' on the Norfolk Broads and Cambridgeshire Fens were, in fact, wind-powered drainage engines connected to scoops or wheels to drain the low-lying marshes into the high-banked rivers. Berney Arms Mill unusually served both functions at different times, having been built originally to grind clinker for the Reedham cement factory and only later being converted to drainage use.

The east of England always had by far the greatest number of windmills in Britain. In Suffolk alone over 500 corn mills were at work in the 1840s, with a further 430 in Norfolk, and as many again are recorded from earlier centuries. So it is hardly surprising that many mills of all types have remained standing to this day, often restored and sometimes back at work producing stone-ground grain for the whole foods market.

Watermills have been in use from Roman times but the sluggish rivers of the eastern counties were not always well suited to water power. However, in the 1200s when returning crusaders

described the windmills they had seen in the Middle East, this new technology was readily taken up by East Anglian millers.

Early structures were small post mills with simple cloth sails. Their heavy mill machinery was contained in a wooden body, known as the buck, balanced on a massive upright oak post that was turned to face into the wind. Saxtead Green Post Mill in Suffolk is a fine example of this type. Parts of its structure may date back to the 18th century, but its height was progressively raised to accommodate additional pairs of stones and, finally, diesel power – a common fate of many former windmills. Smock mills, with a rotating cap above a tall wooden tower (said to resemble a woman's smock) were a later development. Their greater height made them suitable

for drainage work on low-lying ground: the restored Wicken Fen Windpump in Cambridgeshire is a good example.

From the late 18th century onwards, however, brick-built tower mills began to predominate, and this type is most commonly seen throughout the region. In tower mills only the cap and sails rotate, a function performed automatically by a fantail mechanism invented in 1745, that operates through a series of cogs and gears. Windmill sails, too, gradually evolved in design. By the early 1800s canvas sailcloth had largely given way to an ingenious mechanism of shutters, like giant Venetian blinds, which were automatically regulated to catch just enough wind to turn the millstones at a safe and efficient speed.

Above: Inside Saxtead Green Post Mill, Essex

Right: Berney Arms Windmill, Norfolk

NORFOLK & SUFFOLK

Windmills, the enigmatic, reed-choked landscapes of the Broads and the meandering woodland rivers of Constable country: these are powerful images of Norfolk and Suffolk. But East Anglia is more than just a pretty face. These two counties were home to some of the country's most wealthy and influential religious houses, and vast tracts were held by some of medieval England's most powerful men. Notable among these was William de Warenne, the first earl of Surrey and one of the William the Conqueror's right-hand men.

The region's historical interest, of course, easily predates the Norman Conquest. Norfolk was broadly the tribal heartland of the Iceni tribe, who Boudicca led in spectacular revolt against the Romans in 60 AD. The Romans defended their occupation in East Anglia against seafaring barbarians with a number of coastal forts and one, Burgh Castle, is one of the best-preserved Roman monuments in the country. The Saxon Bishops of East Anglia established the centre of their estates at North Elmham, long before the Normans set Bury St Edmunds Abbey on course to becoming the wealthiest and most powerful Benedictine monastery of its day. Many monastic sites became high-status houses after the Dissolution and at some, Thetford among them, this story of continuity is clearly told by the ruins. At the other end of the ecclesiastical scale are sites like St James's Chapel, Lindsey. Like

Opposite: Holkham Bay, Norfolk
Left: Creake Abbey, Norfolk

many others across the region it was reused as a barn in the 16th century, but retains many interesting original features.

Norfolk and Suffolk lacked good building stone and the relatively abundant flint has come to characterise its architecture; indeed the flint mines of Grimes Graves tell us this material has been important for millennia. At Baconsthorpe Castle the Heydon family used galleting to create the fine façade of their home: an intricate inlaying of small flint chips that must have taken an age to execute. Limestone for any but the most basic decoration had to be imported, but only those with the deepest pockets could afford top quality from Caen in Normandy.

From the 13th to the 15th centuries East Anglia prospered. Suffolk was England's weaving capital, and Norfolk's extensive sheep runs put it at the centre of the wool trade. Much of its produce was exported from Blakeney on the north Norfolk coast, whose charm belies its history as one of the region's busiest medieval ports. In the 18th century huge profits were made by agricultural entrepreneurs such as Coke who pioneered the Agricultural Revolution on his estate at Holkham. However, the Industrial Revolution passed East Anglia by. The region lacked the minerals and potential for water-power that favoured other areas and was never wealthy enough to modernise, with the result that its rich legacy of medieval building has survived unscathed by the effects of industrialisation.

Milestone, Norfolk

Blakeney Guildhall

Creake Abbey   Baconsthorpe Castle

Binham Priory   Binham Market Cross

Castle Rising Castle

North Elmham Chapel

Castle Acre Bailey Gate   Castle Acre Castle

Castle Acre Priory

Caister Roman Site

NORFOLK   Cow Tower

Burgh Castle

Berney Arms Windmill   Row III

Grime's Graves

St Olave's Priory

Weeting Castle   Thetford Warren Lodge

Thetford Priory   Church of the Holy Sepulchre

Saxstead Green Post Mill

Bury St Edmunds Abbey

Framlingham Castle   Leiston Abbey

Moulton Packhorse Bridge

SUFFOLK

Orford Castle

Lindsey/St James's Chapel

Landguard Fort

History

Baconsthorpe Castle is, in fact, a fortified manor house, built by successive generations of a prominent Norfolk family – the Heydons. Their building works at Baconsthorpe are not well documented, though it is known that William Heydon acquired the site from the Bacon family in the early 15th century. His son, Sir John, rose to political and social prominence during the Wars of the Roses and probably began the building at Baconsthorpe with the great inner gatehouse, though its exact date is not known. John's son, Sir Henry, completed the moat and the fortified house in its south-west corner later in the 15th century. The 16th century saw another new building phase. With Baconsthorpe well established as part of a vast sheep-run, Sir John Heydon II transformed the east range from accommodation into a textile factory. Around 1560 his successor, Sir Christopher Heydon I, added the outer gatehouse and outer court.

Despite being a successful businessman, Sir Christopher died in debt and his son William had to sell off parts of Baconsthorpe as a result. William's son, also

The 15th-century inner gatehouse. The curtain wall and moat still surround the castle

Christopher, carried out some work on the house, including refitting the gatehouse, but he preferred to live elsewhere. Around the turn of the 17th century the ornamental mere was created on the east arm of the moat, and the formal gardens that have been recorded to the east were also probably created at this time.

Nevertheless, the family fortunes were in decline, and by the mid-17th century the insolvency of successive Heydons had led to the demolition of much of the site. The outer gatehouse survived, however, and was converted into a house known as Baconsthorpe Hall, which remained inhabited until 1920 when one of the turrets fell down.

1588 plan of Baconsthorpe House from the Weybourne forifications, now at Hatfield House

Description

Baconsthorpe is now a peaceful ruin with a water-filled moat. It has an interesting mix of domestic and rather perfunctory defensive elements, reflecting that a castle-like appearance was considered a status symbol long after castles ceased to be built for defence.

The site is approached through the 16th-century outer gatehouse. It is expensively finished in dressed flint and is still an imposing structure despite the loss of one of its octagonal turrets. Interestingly, this was the only part of the castle for which a licence to crenellate was obtained (in 1561), yet it is completely unfortified. The existing embattled entrance is an early 19th-century modification. Beyond the gatehouse are the footings of other rooms relating to its period of use as a house.

Across the outer court the scene is dominated by the earliest castle structure: the massive three-storey inner gatehouse, which is finished with good quality brick and stone dressings. The gate passage was vaulted and there are vaulted lodges to either side, each with a fireplace, cupboard and privy – you can see where the latter drained into the moat. Despite its powerful appearance the gatehouse had large

The finely-finished outer gatehouse was built c 1560

windows and no gunloops. Access across the moat would originally have been by means of a drawbridge; the massive pier that once supported it now carries a modern bridge.

Detail of the outer gatehouse

The remains of the house itself occupy a roughly square platform surrounded on the south, west and north sides by the moat and on the east by the mere. Its flint-rubble walls were originally faced with an ornamental finish of small knapped and squared flints, which survives well in places around the curtain wall. This encloses almost the whole moated area, but differences in its construction indicate it was built in stages, the thickest and earliest section being the south-west angle. The towers give the remains a castle-like feel and the earliest have gunloops, as does the south curtain wall west of the gatehouse (the gunloops to the east are much later and were perhaps added for aesthetic reasons). The northern stretch of wall has larger gunports – for cannon rather than handguns – though the wall itself is relatively insubstantial here. In contrast the later, eastern, stretches of wall have no defensive features and the large window at the south end of the east range is entirely domestic in character. The foundations of the south-west range of the house show that the accommodation was arranged around a courtyard. The east range and the north-east corner tower survive rather better and retain various features related to textile processing. Traces of a turnstile – perhaps for admitting sheep for shearing – have been recorded, and the sunken tank in the now flooded north-east tower was probably used for fulling (thickening) cloth.

¾ mile N of Baconsthorpe off unclassified road, 3 miles E of Holt. OS Map 133, ref TG 121382

History

The history of Binham Priory is one of almost continuous scandal. It was founded in 1091 by Peter de Valoines, nephew of William the Conqueror, as a cell of the Benedictine abbey of St Albans, and was thereafter in the hands of a long list of mainly unscrupulous and irresponsible priors. Prior Richard de Parco appears to have been the exception. Prior from 1227 to 1244, Richard was a diligent man who gained income for the priory and was probably responsible for beginning the magnificent west front. In contrast, and more typical, was the notorious William de Somerton, the prior between 1317 and 1335. Obsessed with the pursuit of his own alchemical experiments, William sold many of the house's valuable items and left the priory £600 in debt. Binham was also

Looking east across the extensive remains of the monastic buildings

subject to almost continual disputes with its mother house, which involved both the king and the Pope. The parishioners also complained, particularly about the monks' monopoly over the use of the church, but it was not until 1432 that a monastic agreement finally reduced parishioners' dues to the priory and introduced regular services. The seven western bays of the nave are now sealed off from the rest and continue to serve as the parish church.

When the priory was suppressed in 1539 its annual income was about £140. Its property was bestowed on a local man, Thomas Paston, who soon began to dismantle the monastic complex to build a house in Wells. His grandson, Edward, carried out further demolition with the intention of building a new house on the site. However, when a workman was killed by falling masonry it was considered such a bad omen that the project was abandoned. It is due to this unfortunate accident that the priory survives to the extent we see today.

Description

Binham Priory is one of the few monastic foundations in Norfolk where the precinct remains essentially intact. The site is entered through the ruins of the largely 15th-century

Binham Priory in the 14th century

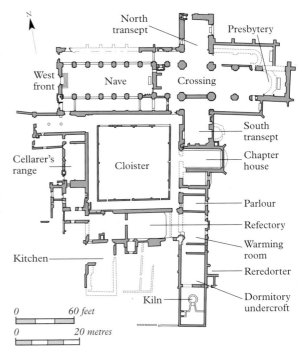

49

gatehouse on the western boundary, and the church's elaborate west front dominates the scene. The large west window has some fine geometrical 'bar tracery': that some have claimed to be one of the earliest examples of its kind in England. The round window at the apex of the design has been restored and its original ironwork is on display inside the church. The lower parts were bricked up by the early 19th century, presumably because this was cheaper than reglazing.

The priory was built of mortared flint rubble, with dressings of Barnack limestone brought from Northamptonshire. The remains of the church are mostly of 12th- and 13th-century date, and you can see that the builders adopted the latest styles as they progressed from east to west. The eastern arcades of the nave are richly decorated with Norman chevrons and cylindrical 'billet' mouldings, while the later, western, arches (inside the church) are pointed and ribbed in Early English style. The priory church was originally cruciform in plan with a central tower supported on massive piers whose bases still retain some of their beautiful decorative mouldings. East of the crossing tower was the presbytery and site of the high altar. The recesses on the outside face of the current east wall are 'putlog' holes, for supporting scaffolding.

The remains of the priory church with the chapter house in the foreground

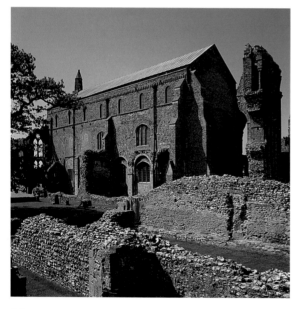

South of the church, the extensive remains of the monastic buildings evoke the daily life of the monks. On the east side of the cloister is the 14th-century chapter house, where the footings for the monks' benches that ran around the sides can still be seen, as well as three of the corner piers that supported its vaulted ceiling. Further south in the same range is the warming room, still with its large fireplace and flanking window seats. West of this, in the south range, is the refectory, and south of this the kitchen with ovens and a kiln. The remains of the monks' washing place can be seen at the south-west angle of the cloister. Adjoining this complex are the earthwork remains of the priory's agricultural buildings and enclosures and beyond these,

The west front, 1820 engraving by W Woolnoth

bordering the stream, is the site of its mill and fishponds.

Inside the church you can see the remains of the ancient rood screen, originally located at the site of the current east wall. It was painted over after the Reformation with texts from Cranmer's bible of 1539. Other features of interest include the octagonal font with its sculptured panels of the sacraments, two beautifully decorated misericord seats and the fine oak benches each carved with a different design.

¼ mile NW of Binham-on-Wells on road off B1388.
OS Map 132, ref TF 982399.
Tel 01328 830434

51

BINHAM MARKET CROSS

History

Over 12,000 standing crosses are thought to have been erected throughout England from the mid-10th to mid-16th centuries. In churchyards they served as stations for outdoor processions, and within settlements as places for preaching, public proclamation and penance, as well as defining rights of sanctuary. They were also employed to mark boundaries between parishes, property or settlements and sometimes to commemorate battles. Some crosses were linked to particular saints whose support and protection their presence would help to invoke. Many cross-heads were destroyed by iconoclasts during the 16th and 17th centuries and now less than 2,000 examples, with or without cross-heads, are thought to survive.

On Binham village green adjacent to the priory.
OS Map 132, ref TF 984396

Description

Binham Market Cross is one of the best surviving examples of a medieval standing cross in Norfolk. It stands on the green in the centre of the village and could have been erected by the monks of nearby Binham Priory. Following the granting of a charter by Henry I an annual fair and a weekly market were held here from the early 1100s, and fairs continued to be held on the green until the early 1950s. The 15th-century cross is built of Barnack limestone and has a socket stone and separate shaft. The 2m-tall base on which these stand is of mortared flint rubble with stepped courses of stone blocks, capped by a platform of thin slabs. You can see that some of the stone blocks have been reused. The weathered remains of an ornamental moulding can still be seen partway up the shaft, but the stone cross that originally topped the shaft is missing.

History

The picturesque village of Blakeney was the third most important port in Norfolk when the Guildhall was built in the 15th century, yet few buildings survive from this prosperous period. The Guildhall's flint and stone construction reflects its own importance and that of Blakeney itself. It may originally have been a merchant's house but was home to Blakeney's guild of fish merchants by 1516 when they were granted a charter by Henry VIII. The building subsequently had a surprising variety of uses. It is shown on a map of 1682 with a castellated upper storey though this part of the building, perhaps used as an inn, later fell into disrepair. In the mid-19th century the undercroft was used for storing coal that was traded along the coast between Newcastle and London, but by the end of the 19th century the haven began to silt up and the port rapidly declined. In the First World War the Guildhall served as a temporary mortuary for shipwrecked sailors.

Description

Set just back from the quayside, the Guildhall was probably originally entered from the higher ground to the south. The surviving undercroft itself has attractive ribbed brick vaulting supported by a central row of octagonal stone columns. It has rendered walls and a cobbled floor, and was lit by three windows in the east wall. Climb the slope to get a better view of the ruined upper storey; at the south-east corner are the remains of a brick-lined privy chute from the upper level and a spiral stairway to the undercroft.

Above: Blakeney Guildhall

Below left: The undercroft

In Blakeney off A149.
OS Map 133, ref TG 028441

The Roman sites at Burgh and Caister-on-Sea were part of a string of forts along what the Romans knew as the 'Saxon Shore', the stretch of coast extending between the Solent and the Wash. These 'Saxon Shore forts' are thought to have acted as a defensive system against seaborne raiders, and would have been naval bases and perhaps defended trading centres. They were under the command of the Count of the Saxon Shore and are documented in the *Notitia Dignitatum*, an official list of all military commands at the end of the 4th century AD. This tells us that Burgh was home to the Stablesian cavalry unit, and cropmarks out-side the walls indicate there was an extensive *vicus* or civilian settle-ment there. In the 4th century AD Burgh and Caister controlled the entrance to the Waveney estuary, which is occupied by extensive marshes. They probably operated together and one, or both, were known by the Romans as Gariannonum. For more than half a century the Saxon raids were checked fairly successfully and it was not until 367 AD, when the Saxons, Picts and Scots made a concerted attack on Britain, that the forts began to be overrun and the Count was killed.

Bede records that in about 630 AD Sigeberht, king

The impressive walls of Burgh Castle. The fort originally covered 6 acres

of the East Angles, gave land inside a Roman fortress to St Fursa to found a monastery. The site, which was call Cnobheresburh, may have been Burgh: there is evidence for Saxon occupation and a cemetery inside the fort at this time. However Caister is also a likely candidate. It too was the site of Saxon activity from the 7th century, and there was a large Saxon cemetery to the south of the fort.

It is worth visiting both sites to get a good impression of these Roman forts: Burgh for its still imposing defences and striking location; and Caister for the evidence of its internal streets and buildings.

BURGH CASTLE

Burgh Castle is one of the best preserved Roman monuments in the country. Built in the late 3rd century AD on a low cliff above the Waveney estuary, its substantial walls are an impressive sight. Today the main route into the fort is the eastern gate. The west wall has long since tumbled into the marshes, with the result that

The collapsed south wall with Breydon Water and Berney Arms Windmill beyond

the drama of entering the fort is increased by the panoramic view across Breydon Water.

Originally enclosing an area of about six acres, the walls of the fort were around 3.5m wide at the base and taper to 1.5m at their full height of around 4.5m. They were further fortified, at a late stage in the construction, by projecting towers or bastions. Each has a central circular hole, either for anchoring catapults called *ballistae* or to support timber watchtowers that may have been linked along the top of the walls. You can see this feature more clearly on the bastion that has fallen outward from the south wall.

55

Over the centuries the walls have been plundered for building material, exposing the mortared flint rubble core, but they were originally faced inside and out with cut flint and tile in alternating bands. A well-preserved stretch of this facing survives along the outside of the south wall. Inside the south wall and at the north-east corner of the fort are the remains of deep socket holes, probably the site of lean-to buildings or gantries, but other than this little is known of the fort's interior layout.

After the Norman conquest Burgh was used as a motte-and-bailey castle; the walls formed the bailey and a motte and ditch were constructed in the south-west corner. You can clearly see where the ditch has breached the south wall, though the mound itself has long since been levelled. In the 19th century, quarrying for the nearby brickworks further ate into the western edge of the fort; the now reed-filled wharf that

Reconstruction of the South Gate of the fort at Caister in the 3rd century AD

once served the brickworks lies just to the south-west.

CAISTER ROMAN SITE

In Roman times the fort at Caister-on-Sea stood on rising land at the edge of a wide estuary, with water on its east and south sides. It was built before Burgh Castle, in the late 2nd or early 3rd centuries AD and, unlike its partner across the water, its defensive wall was backed by an earthen rampart but had no external bastions. The roughly square site

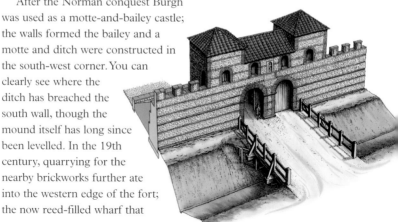

enclosed about seven acres and was further defended on all four sides by ditches, now mostly infilled. The estuary over which Caister once presided has greatly silted up and modern housing now covers most of the fort, but sections of the outer wall and ditch and the remains of some of the buildings can be seen.

The foundations of the building at Caister, showing the remains of the hypocaust

As you enter the site the foundations of a guardroom and a section of the inner ditch are to your left; this ditch would originally have been around 5m wide. The interior of the fort was probably subdivided by a grid pattern of streets, although only two of these have been located by excavation. The footings you can see relate to one or two buildings. Evidence of a hypocaust heating system is visible in one of the rooms; stacks of tiles originally supported the floor under which hot air circulated. The buildings would have been timber framed and decorated inside with painted plaster.

The many finds from the site include a coin hoard, which may have been a soldier's savings, and uniform fittings suggesting that Caister, like Burgh, was home to a cavalry unit. As well as military items, numerous personal ornaments were found including brooches, a soapstone bowl and a bronze figure of a dog, possibly the Egyptian god Anubis. Other finds, hair pins for example, indicate that women were living at the fort from at least the late 3rd century. Personal effects like these tell us that Caister was more than just a military base.

Burgh is at far W end of Breydon Water on unclassified road, 3 miles W of Great Yarmouth. *OS Map 134, ref TG 475047.* Caister is near Caister-on-Sea, 3 miles N of Great Yarmouth. *OS Map 134, ref TG 517123*

Castle Acre is a remarkable Norman settlement. It was once a fortified town bounded by a substantial earthen bank and ditch and had two well-defended gateways. To the south-east of the village are the remains of Castle Acre Priory, the best-preserved Cluniac monastery in the country. To the north-east are the ruins of the castle, founded just after the Norman Conquest by William de Warenne, first earl of Surrey. Several generations of de Warennes were intimately involved in affairs of state and a number of English kings are known to have been entertained here.

THE CASTLE

The quiet Norfolk landscape provides few naturally defensible sites, but Castle Acre Castle makes the best of its position on gently rising ground, dominating the ancient Peddars Way where it crosses the River Nar. The castle was the focal point of the Warenne family's Norfolk estates. Its principal building was essentially a country house, but in the 12th century the castle's defences were greatly strengthened and a remarkable reconstruction turned the house into a keep. The site probably became derelict late in the 14th century, but its earthworks are among the most impressive to survive in Britain.

Despite their power and influence, the Warenne family's hold over Castle Acre was not uninterrupted. John Warenne, the last of the direct family

The castle, Bailey Gate and town defences of Castle Acre

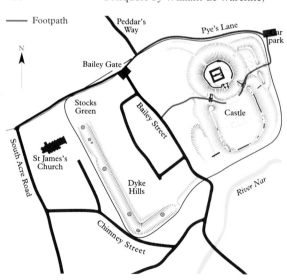

— Footpath

Peddar's Way

Pye's Lane

Car park

Bailey Gate

N

Stocks Green

Bailey Street

Castle

St James's Church

South Acre Road

Dyke Hills

River Nar

Chimney Street

line, was excommunicated for adultery in 1316. The same year he gave the castle and town of Castle Acre to Aymer de Valence, Earl of Pembroke and Ambassador to the Pope, probably to help press his suit for divorce. In 1317 Warenne helped the Earl of Lancaster's wife to elope. Enraged, Lancaster seized much of Warenne's northern estates and for the next two years a private war waged between the two. Warenne did not recover all of his possessions until 1326, four years after Lancaster's execution, but several more years' of complicated legal transactions were required before Castle Acre finally returned to the Warenne family. By this time the castle was probably derelict: a survey in 1397 gave its value as nil. The last earl's unsettled life and a series of absentee landlords had taken their toll. From then on the castle was of value only for its agricultural land and as a convenient source of building material for the townspeople. Nevertheless, the site continued to change hands over the centuries. In

Castle Acre Castle dominates the surrounding countryside

1615 Sir Edward Coke acquired the manor and site of the dissolved monastery and the castle remains the possession of his descendants.

Description

The earthworks of the castle are particularly impressive, with formidable banks and ditches defending the outer and inner wards. If you approach the site from the east you will cross the barbican, which guarded the eastern access to the castle and was defended by its own moat. It was originally linked to the main castle defences by substantial walls across the outer moat, remains of which can be seen to the south. Beyond are the remains of the eastern gateway. It was not particularly heavily defended, presumably relying on the protection of the barbican to which it was linked by a timber bridge. Approaching from the village you enter through the western gateway, which survives rather better and provided the original access between the castle and the town. The bases of its twin drum towers remain together with the grooves for a pair of doors and a portcullis. The small vaulted chamber inside the bank was probably a storeroom. Around the top of the bank you can see sections of the curtain wall that originally surrounded the lower ward. This and the

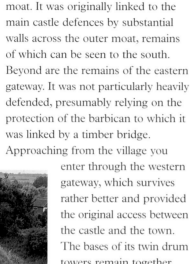

The western gateway was the main access to the castle in the 13th century

eastern gateway are of 12th-century date; the western gateway was added later that century or early in the 13th. The rectangular earthworks at the centre of the lower ward mark the foundations of a great hall and kitchen, probably accommodation for guests, with a probable chapel to the north.

Access to the upper ward was by means of a gatehouse built almost entirely of chalk. Little remains above ground, however the considerable width of the passageway suggests it was built more for show than for strength (in the mid-12th century the rear archway was narrowed to admit only pedestrians). The original 'country house' was built some time around 1070–85. The main accommodation in the house would have been on the first floor, and in the better-preserved north half of the building you can see the remains of a curved fireplace flue in the north wall and part of a window to the west. The 12th-century conversion involved the addition of substantially thicker walls within those of the house; the junction between these phases can be seen in the foundations of the south wall. The strengthening of the defences also involved heightening the original low bank around the house, and the construction of a curtain wall. The north side of the bank was heightened a second time and a flint wall was built on top of the first. This effectively buried the lower floor of the house, turning it into a basement for the keep.

THE BAILEY GATE

This gateway was in fact the northern entrance to the village of Castle Acre and not a gate to the castle bailey, though it is similar in plan to the castle's western gateway with which it is presumably contemporary. The main road into the village still runs between its towers and it is a prominent landmark in the centre of

The Bailey Gate once guarded the northern entrance to the town of Castle Acre

the village. The gate is rectangular in plan and has solid, twin drum towers faced with knapped flint. The bases of the towers are battered – they slope outwards as protection from undermining. In the arched gate passage the rebates for the two sets of double doors and the sockets for their draw-bars are visible, along with grooves for the portcullis.

Farther south, at the foot of what is now Bailey Street, a similar gateway was demolished in the early 19th century. These gateways, together with the perimeter earthworks, the castle and the grid pattern of streets, are the hallmarks of a planned medieval town. To view the town ditch, walk down Priory Road from the Bailey Gate and turn left along the footpath to the churchyard.

Castle Acre is 5 miles N of Swaffham. OS Map 132, Castle ref TF 819152; Bailey Gate ref TF 817151 Castle is at E end of village; Bailey Gate is in the centre.

East Anglia has been the birthplace and inspiration of many writers and artists, and the landscapes of Suffolk's Stour Valley provided the backdrop for two great artists: Thomas Gainsborough and John Constable. Gainsborough was born in Sudbury in 1727 and achieved great fame as both a portrait and landscape painter. The house where he was born is open to the public and has a large collection of his work. Half a century later, in 1776, Constable was born farther down the valley in East Bergholt. One of his best-known paintings is of Flatford Mill, which was owned by his wealthy corn-merchant father. The countryside had fascinated Constable since childhood and he studied the natural world closely in order to paint in a realistic style that was not fashion-able at the start of his career.

In the early 19th century, as Constable was achieving some recognition, a group of painters in neighbouring Norfolk were forming the Norwich Society. Lead by John Crome (1768–1821) and John Sell Cotman (1782–1842), their subjects were mainly landscapes and coastal scenes from around Norfolk. The Society's annual exhibitions were the first of their kind outside London. Both Crome and Cotman were prolific painters – Cotman mostly in watercolour and Crome in oils. Today, Norwich School paintings can often be identified by their reddish-brown tint as the indigo blue pigment they favoured has faded over time.

Above: Gainsborough's house in Sudbury, 46 Gainsborough Street

Left: Mr and Mrs Andrews, c1748–9, by Gainsborough

the 18th century William Wordsworth and Samuel Taylor Coleridge studied there and in 1827 Tennyson followed his hero Byron to Trinity College. Tennyson was living in Epping, Essex, in the 1840s when he published some of his finest work, including a revision of *The Lady of Shalott*.

Victorian novelist H Rider Haggard was inspired by his work and travels in Africa, but his colourful adventure novels, including *King Solomon's Mines* and *She*, were written after his retirement to his native Norfolk. Great Yarmouth-born Anna Sewell wrote just one book, but *Black Beauty*, published in 1878, became a classic loved by children and adults alike.

The east of England was also the home of Julian of Norwich, the first woman to write a book in English: *The Revelations of Divine Love*. This 14th-century work is regarded by many as a spiritual classic. Another deeply religious writer, John Bunyan, was born near Bedford in 1628. He preached widely in the 1650s but was imprisoned for his views after the Restoration, and it was in Bedford Prison that he began *The Pilgrim's Progress*. Published in 1678, the book became a centre-piece of Protestant literature; the 'Palace Beautiful' he describes is believed to be Houghton House in Bedfordshire.

Cambridge University has nurtured many men of words, including 17th-century poets John Milton and Andrew Marvell. In

Today the region is at the forefront of literary activity with the University of East Anglia's famed MA in Creative Writing. UEA graduates include Ian McEwan, Rose Tremain and Kazuo Ishiguro.

Above: Hadleigh Castle, 1829, by John Constable
Right: Alfred, Lord Tennyson

History

The Priory of the Holy Sepulchre was founded in about 1148 by William de Warenne, as home to a community of Canons of the Holy Sepulchre. It was then one of only six such houses in the country, and today these unassuming ruins are the only standing remains in England of this small independent religious order. The canons were all ordained priests and the order derived from one founded in Jerusalem that aimed to provide aid to pilgrims visiting the supposed site of Christ's burial.

Before William de Warenne departed on crusade he endowed the priory with the Church of St Sepulchre and an area of adjoining land, together with all the lands, churches, tithes and manorial rights that he held south of the river in Thetford. Despite these, and further grants from the Crown and de Warenne's successors, the house was never wealthy and records suggest that it declined in later years. During the later medieval period the recorded number of brethren in the community ranged from eight to just three. After the suppression of the priory the nave of the church survived and was used as a barn, but by the 18th century the east end had been demolished. In the 19th century the ruins were adapted as an ornamental garden feature with a grotto.

The church is all that remains of the 12th-century priory. The remains of a 19th-century flint grotto are in the foreground

Description

The flint-rubble church nave is all that remains of the priory. Its south, west and north walls have survived to nearly roof height though they have lost most of their architectural detail. The nave is rectangular and without aisles. Foundations revealed by limited excavations to the east and north show that the church was originally around 53m long and cruciform in plan, with rectangular transepts to the north and south of a central crossing. The small priory followed the conventional pattern, with the church on an east–west axis and the cloister and monastic buildings to one side, in this case on the north. None of these are visible today.

The entrance to the church itself is now through the east wall, through an 18th-century doorway that incorporates a large amount of reused stone – you can see sections of decorative mouldings set into it. The door at the far end of the north wall was originally the door to the canons' cloister, indicating that this was a

The cart door is a reminder of the church's use as a barn

priory church rather than a simple parish one. Further evidence for this is provided by what is left of the windows. On the south wall they are large and low, as they would be in a parish church, but on the north wall the remains of the windows are much higher up, in order to clear the cloister roof on the other side. A barn door has been inserted into the south side of the church, and the remains of an apse-ended cart shed can be seen to the south of the ruins. The now ruinous 19th-century grotto, which originally had a domed roof, is attached to the south-east corner of the church.

On W side of Thetford, off B1107 (parking on grass, directly off this busy road).
OS Map 144, ref TL 865831

65

The Cow Tower played a key role in Norwich's medieval defences

History

The Cow Tower stands on a bend in the River Yare, at the north-east corner of what was at one time a low lying meadow known as Cowholme – which perhaps accounts for its name – within the precinct of St Giles's hospital (now the Great Hospital). The tower was originally built as a river tollhouse for one of the monastic orders, but was later given to the Great Hospital. In a ruinous condition in 1378, it was rebuilt as one of the series of blockhouses or artillery towers that formed Norwich's city defences. It would have housed guns and a garrison of gunners to defend the approach across the river, and its strategic position on a bend of the river allowed it to command the high ground on the opposite bank.

The tower you see today was built towards the end of the 14th century. Its construction is exceptionally well documented in the Great Hospital's accounts for the year 1398–9: these include days worked and the costs of materials and workmen, which show

that little expense was spared on this building which would have been a showpiece of its time. There are further documentary references relating to the tower's maintenance and repair as part of the city's defences during the 15th century. Twenty-seven artillery towers are known to survive in various states of repair, some now incorporated into later military constructions. The Cow Tower is believed to be one of the earliest blockhouses to have been built and is a fine example of the use of brick in the medieval period.

Description

The Cow Tower is an impressive structure, with its solid, 2m-thick walls and massive battlements. The walls of the tower have a core of mortared flint rubble that was faced internally and externally with brick and had external stone dressings. In places the walls stand almost to their full original height which was 15m above the present ground level. Some of the finest brickwork can be seen in the jambs of the doorways and fireplaces, and around the outlets of the garderobes. The wider gaps in the battlements – the crenels – were designed for cannon to be fired through, while the narrower loops were for early light-calibre hand guns or crossbows. The clever arrangement of these provided overlapping fields of fire. Larger guns could also have been mounted on the roof platform.

Although the roof and internal floors are long gone, you can get some idea of their position from the threshold of a door, a fireplace at second-floor level and from wall openings on the outside of the building. The ground floor with its large fireplace was probably a mess room, while the two floors above may have served as sleeping quarters.

Boat Builder's Yard, near the Cow's Tower, Norwich, c1812, by Norwich School painter John Thirtle

In Norwich, on the bank of the River Yare along the riverside walk, accessible from Bishopsgate and the Cathedral. OS Map 134, ref TG 240092. Tel 01603 212343

CREAKE ABBEY

History

Creake Abbey probably had its origins in 1206 when Sir Robert and Lady Alice de Nerford established the small chapel of St Mary of the Meadows at Lingerescroft, bordering the tiny River Burn. In 1217 they founded the Hospital of St Bartholomew there and when the establishment embraced the rule of St Augustine the chapel became a priory, prompting extensions to both the church and priory buildings.

In 1225 Henry III elevated the priory to abbey status and it benefited from many generous donations, but a fire in around 1484 left the abbot at Creake petitioning the king for help. Despite gifts from Richard III and a bequest by Sir William Calthorpe, the nave and parts of the transepts were demolished, reducing the house once more to a modest church. Early in the 16th century the abbey was devastated by the plague and when the abbot died, alone, on 12 December 1506, the abbey reverted to the Crown.

Description

Creake Abbey has remained a tranquil spot and the attractive ruins tell the tale of the abbey's varying fortunes. What survives are the remains of the abbey church – the presbytery, crossing, north transept and parts of the north and south chapels – while the nave remains only as low walls and foundations. The mid-13th-century presbytery was the earliest structure on the site, to which the chapels, transepts and crossing were added later in the 13th century. The nave is also later 13th century; its

The remains of the crossing arch hint at the original scale of the abbey church

south wall was refaced in post-medieval times and is now the garden wall of an adjacent private house.

Early in the 14th century the north transept chapels were rebuilt on a larger scale and much 13th-

View of Creake Abbey, 1738, by Samuel and Nathaniel Buck

century stonework was reused in the rebuilding of the arches between the transept and the chapels. The chapels each have a piscina, where the priest washed the sacred vessels, and the arched recess in the north chapel probably once housed a tomb. The smaller, inner chapel has an aumbry or cupboard. During the excavation of this part of the church considerable areas of external plasterwork were found on the north and east walls of the chapel.

The hardships of the 15th century reduced the abbey church to the size of a chapel. The nave walls were taken down, probably to the level you see today, and the south arches to the crossing and transepts were blocked to create a new west wall. The eastern processional doorway from the cloister was blocked, and the western door was reset to face north into what had become an open space. The majority of the north transept was sacrificed and, as it was now outside the roofed area of the church, the original doorway to the spiral stair in its north-east corner was blocked. You can see where a new doorway was forced into the stairs from the chapel to the east. The south-facing, 15th-century window in the south chapel overlooks the site of the south transept, suggesting that it too probably ceased to be roofed at this time.

N of North Creake off B1355. OS Map 132, ref TF 856395

14th-century defensive earthworks still surround the remains of the chapel, seen here from the south east

History

North Elmham is an enigmatic site with an interesting history. The ruins are those of a small Norman chapel of unique design, which was converted into a small castle whose defensive banks and moats still surround the site. In the late Saxon period North Elmham was the principal seat of the Bishops of East Anglia and the centre of a great episcopal estate. Excavations have revealed evidence for an earlier timber structure, probably the Anglo-Saxon cathedral, which went out of use when the seat of the Bishop was transferred to Thetford in 1071. Some time between 1091 and 1119 Bishop Herbert de Losinga founded a new parish church for the village and built a small private chapel for his own use on the site of the old timber church.

In the 14th century Bishop Henry le Despencer held the manor of North Elmham. He turned the chapel into a house and in 1388 obtained a royal licence to fortify. He was not a popular man, especially in Norfolk where he was despised for his merciless quashing of the Peasants' Revolt, and this fortification suggests he felt ill at ease among his tenants. There is no record of any bishop occupying the site after Henry's death in 1406 though manorial courts continued to be held there. When Elmham passed into the hands of the notorious Thomas Cromwell the 'castle' site was assigned to the vicarage and gradually fell into ruin.

Description

The conversion of the chapel into a fortified house makes the ruins rather difficult to interpret at first sight. The rather eccentric design of the chapel reflects that of much grander European churches of the period. Unusually, the west tower was the same width externally as the nave and had an external stair turret to its upper storeys. The transept had flanking towers, reminiscent of contemporary German churches, and there was a semi-circular apse at the east end. The church was built mainly of blocks

of local, dark brown conglomerate with courses of large flints and limestone dressings; most of these have been robbed but remaining ashlar fragments have distinctively Norman diagonal tooling. The towers can be distinguished by having slightly thicker walls than the nave and transepts. The north support for the tower arch and the surviving jamb of the north doorway are also clearly Norman in design.

Bishop Despencer's 14th-century alterations are mostly of small flints with brick and ashlar dressings. The foundations you can see at ground level are the remains of his cellars and the circular bases of the piers that supported a new upper floor. The existing flight of stairs led up to the living rooms and hall. Despencer created a fortified first-floor entrance by building a second semicircular turret alongside the Norman stair turret. He surrounded his house with a moat, and the bailey to the north and east, and outer ditch around the west, north and east sides, are probably also his work.

Above: The south door of the chapel

Left: North Elmham Chapel as it might have looked c1100

6 miles N of
East Dereham
on B1110.
*OS Map 132,
ref TF 988216*

History

The Priory of Our Lady of Thetford has a colourful history, and remains today an attractive ruin with an exceptionally well-preserved gatehouse. It belonged to the Order of Cluny, a rich and powerful Benedictine monastery in Burgundy, and was founded in 1103 by Roger Bigod, friend and counsellor of William the Conqueror. The priory was first established in the town of Thetford but when this proved too cramped

The east end of the nave and remains of the crossing arch are among the earliest elements of the priory church

the second prior, Stephen, obtained authority to move to the site on which the ruins now stand. Work was begun on 1 September 1107 but Bigod died a week later and it was not until 1114 that the priory occupied its new church. The construction of the other monastic buildings continued throughout the rest of the 12th century.

In the 13th century, according to legend, a local craftsman suffering from an incurable disease prayed incessantly to the Virgin Mary for the restoration of his health. She appeared to him in a vision, asking that a chapel be built for her on the north side of the priory church. After the third repetition of his vision the man told the prior, who was so impressed that he gave orders for a wooden chapel to be built. However, when the craftsman returned to him and said it was Our Lady's wish that the chapel should be of stone, the prior ignored him. Only when a Thetford woman had a similar vision was the prior finally convinced; he then built the stone Lady Chapel, setting up over its altar the old, stone image of Our Lady, cleaned and redecorated. During the redecoration the statue was found to have a hollow in its head containing certain relics of saints. These conferred miraculous powers of healing on the statue and it was not long before the news of this spread around the countryside and pilgrims flocked to Thetford from all directions, hoping to be healed of various ailments. This cult brought considerable financial profit to the priory, and before the end of the 13th century the whole east end of the church was rebuilt on a more elaborate scale.

The story is not entirely one of prosperity, however, and the community incurred a substantial debt from the king's demands from French-based priories during the wars with France. In 1376, however, Edward III recognised the priory as 'denizen' – giving it the same rights as an English foundation – for the sum of £100, and towards the end of the 14th century the community was once again able to carry out repairs and alterations to its buildings.

Thetford Priory

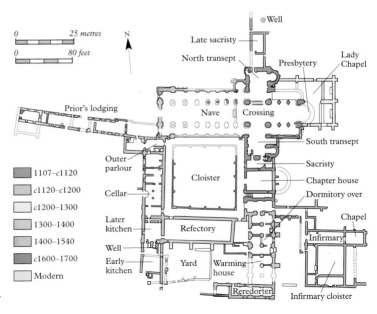

▆	1107–*c*1120
▨	*c*1120–*c*1200
☐	*c*1200–1300
▩	1300–1400
▨	1400–1540
▆	*c*1600–1700
☐	Modern

0   25 metres
0   80 feet

N

Well

Late sacristy
North transept
Presbytery
Lady Chapel

Prior's lodging
Nave   Crossing

South transept

Outer parlour
Cloister
Sacristy
Chapter house
Dormitory over

Cellar

Later kitchen
Refectory
Chapel

Well
Yard   Warming house
Infirmary

Early kitchen
Reredorter
Infirmary cloister

On the death of the last Roger Bigod in 1306 the family's Norfolk estates passed to the Crown and then to the Dukes of Norfolk. When, in 1536, the priory was threatened with suppression the staunchly Catholic duke petitioned King Henry VIII to convert it into a college of secular canons. He pointed out that he was preparing in the church not only his own tomb – beside his ancestors – but also one for the King's own son: Henry Fitzroy, Duke of Richmond, Henry's illegitimate son by Lady Elizabeth Blount. The duke's petition failed, and on 16 February 1540 the last prior and 16 monks surrendered to the King's Commissioners. Some time after the Dissolution the tomb of Thomas Howard, victor of Flodden, was moved to Framlingham, though its site is still marked in the nave at Thetford. The prior's lodging was converted into a high status house and the priory itself fell into ruin.

Blocked window in the prior's lodging

Description

Construction of the church began in 1107 and the eastern parts were probably complete by 1114 when the community moved to the site. Enough remains of the west front to show that it was decorated with arcading and had two flanking towers; the remains of the stairs into both can still be seen. The nave is very ruinous and of the 14 piers that once supported the main arcades parts of only six survive. There is a small difference in the width of the nave bays – the four western ones are two feet (0.6 m) wider than the eastern four – indicating different building campaigns. Between the seventh pair of piers are the remains of the rood screen and nave altar – the original chalk altar has not survived the elements and is reconstructed in stone. One of the supporting piers for the crossing tower survives to a considerable height, and high up you can still see a beautifully carved corbel from which springs a fragment of the crossing arch. Further east is the high altar, and the site of Thomas Howard's tomb.

The ruins of the extensive monastic complex extend southwards from the church. East of the cloister, the chapter house still has the remains of the monks' bench around its walls and the bases of its supporting columns. West of the church is the prior's lodging, a long two-storey range that contained accommodation for the prior or his guests on the upper floor. The large, square windows, themselves mostly blocked, date from its conversion to a house in the 16th century when many stone features were reused, for instance in its fine arched entrances. The grassed area to the south of the lodging was once the Victorian kitchen garden for nearby Abbey House.

Follow the sign through the gate to the north west of the priory, past Abbey House, to the 14th-century gatehouse. Although now divorced from the rest of the complex this would have guarded the main approach to the priory, leading directly to the prior's lodging. The three-storey gatehouse stands intact

except for its floors, roof and parapets and remains virtually unmodified. It has octagonal turrets at the south-east and south-west corners and is faced with knapped flint with stone dressings. Scars from old roof lines show where other structures once adjoined it. West of the gatehouse, beyond the current boundary of the site, stand two of the priory's original barns; dating to around 1430, these are the only surviving inner precinct monastic barns in the country.

16th-century windows in the prior's lodging attest its continued use

On W side of Thetford near the station.
OS Map 144, ref TL 866834

75

The substantial lodge was a high status building in the 15th century

History

This interesting lodge was probably built around 1400 by the prior of Our Lady's Priory, Thetford. The prior had the right of free warren – a licence from the king to hunt small game – and the area would have been an obvious target for armed poachers. The many defensive features incorporated into his lodge show that the prior took this threat seriously. This is a substantial stone building and, in an area where stone and brick were costly materials, clearly demonstrates the wealth and social standing of its owner. The quality of the building work inside and out also indicates that the lodge was intended to accommodate hunting parties as well as the prior's gamekeeper.

After the final dissolution of Thetford Priory in 1540 the monastic lands were granted to the Duke of Norfolk, who had been its patron. Until the early years of the 20th century the area surrounding the lodge was one of the most productive rabbit warrens in the Breckland region of Norfolk. It is known that the warreners who managed and culled the stock occupied Thetford Warren Lodge from at least the 18th century onwards. They made alterations to the building and used the rooms on the ground floor for drying rabbit skins and storing their traps, nets and lanterns. The lodge was later incorporated into a farmhouse, which was abandoned after a fire.

Description

Thetford Warren Lodge retains many original features and is a rare example of its kind. It is a rectangular tower-house built of mortared flint rubble and reused stones, some of which are reddened and were probably removed from the nearby priory after a fire. The walls were substantial – up to 1m thick at floor level – and stand for the most part to almost their original height. The limestone dressings also include many reused 12th-century architectural fragments. The level of the upper storey is marked by an offset

on the interior face of the walls. The lodge had numerous defensive features, including a parapet from which the gamekeeper could look out over what was then open country. The lower windows are narrow loops and the single entrance has a *meutrière* or murder-hole – a chute over the porch down which missiles and boiling liquids could be delivered onto unwelcome visitors. Inside the house the remains of an internal staircase and two fireplaces can be seen. There is also a partial intermediate floor at a lower level with sluices in the wall, possibly a suspended game-larder.

The south-eastern angle of the building has been rebuilt and the repair is clearly marked by the inclusion of random ashlar and brick in the fabric. The roof is modern.

'Pillow mounds', like this one depicted in the 14th-century Luttrell Psalter, were built for the rabbits by the warreners

2 miles W of Thetford off B1107.
OS Map 144, ref TL 839841

History

This small Augustinian priory was founded by Roger FitzOsbert in around 1216. It is dedicated to Olaf, 11th-century king and patron saint of Norway whose stark Christian message was 'baptism or death'. An inventory taken in 1536 records little of value and the house was probably already in decline when it was suppressed a year later. In 1547 Sir Henry Jerningham converted the buildings to the north of the cloister into a private house but little of this survived when the priory was dismantled in 1784. Around 1825 the floor of the refectory undercroft was raised and the building was converted into a cottage which was occupied until 1902.

Description

The hidden gem in this unassuming ruin is its 14th-century refectory undercroft. Its vaulted brick ceiling is an important early example of the use of brick in England. Supported on Purbeck marble columns, it is still almost complete and retains much of its original plasterwork.

The only parts of the church to survive are a stretch of the south aisle, the west wall and parts of the north wall. The foundations of some of the brick-faced piers that supported the cloister arcade are visible, but nothing remains of the west range except the flintwork cloister wall, which is pierced near the north end by a 14th-century doorway. At the back of the refectory is a fragment of Jerningham's 16th-century house that escaped destruction, which includes a reused 14th-century doorway.

The undercroft with its fine brick vaulting

5½ miles SW of
Great Yarmouth
on A143.
*OS Map 134,
ref TM 459996*

History

The manor of Weeting was owned by the de Warenne family from the late 11th century and was held by the de Plais family from the early 12th century, when Hugh de Plais built Weeting Castle. Weeting is a typical example of an East Anglian medieval great house. The de Plais remained in residence until about 1390 when the castle seems to have gone out of use. It was then passed through a number of families and in 1775 it ended up in the hands of the Earl of Mountrath, who built Weeting Hall some time before 1794.

Description

Today Weeting Castle is ruinous, but parts of the southern tower and the south end of the hall still stand three-storeys high. The rectangular hall was built of mortared flint rubble with stone dressings. It was converted in the mid-12th century to an aisled hall, a form that remained common throughout the Middle Ages, and scars from internal timbers suggest

Now ruinous, Weeting Castle was a typical East Anglian great house in the 12th century

that it was divided into three bays. The hall was substantial, with walls up to 1m thick, and would have been the public and administrative centre of the manor. The moat was added during the early 14th century, as a status symbol rather than a defensive feature, and excavations have shown that a square kitchen was added to the north of the hall at about the same time.

On the moated island is a fine example of a late 18th-century, brick-built icehouse, located to take advantage of the ready supply of ice from the moat.

2 miles N of Brandon off B1106.
OS Map 144, ref TL 778891

Since the first days of powered flight no part of Britain has seen so much activity in its air space as East Anglia. Its flat landscape, sparse population and lack of major urban centres or industrial obstructions made the siting of airfields relatively easy. By the outbreak of war in 1914 aircraft were already operating out of places like Felixstowe, Great Yarmouth and Thetford; by 1917 new sites included the bomber base at Bircham Newton, the training station at Duxford and the airship base at Pulham Market, home of the huge airships known locally as Pulham Pigs.

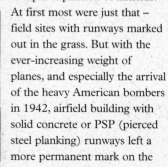

Above: The hangar at Duxford, Cambridgeshire, constructed in 1917 and now a museum

Right: RAF Neatishead, Norfolk. Type 84 radar

Expansion began in earnest from 1934. This was the year when Mildenhall base opened with a blaze of publicity for the start of the Mildenhall to Melbourne Air Race. Home to RAF Wellington bombers during the war, Mildenhall was taken over by the United States Air Force in 1946 and now serves as their principal depot for huge transport planes. But the Second World War saw the most rapid expansion of airfields.

At first most were just that – field sites with runways marked out in the grass. But with the ever-increasing weight of planes, and especially the arrival of the heavy American bombers in 1942, airfield building with solid concrete or PSP (pierced steel planking) runways left a more permanent mark on the countryside. By 1945 there were 107 operational air bases in East Anglia from which over 5,000 flights took off every day. The brave fighter pilots of Duxford and Debden played a crucial role in repulsing the planned German invasion in the 1940 Battle of Britain.

Wherever you are in the eastern counties you are rarely more than ten miles from a former or current airbase. They are undoubtedly amongst our most numerous and significant historical sites, though often little appreciated. English Heritage has undertaken a major recording exercise, detailing their surviving buildings and features. So what remains of our abandoned airfields?

Most grass runways have long since returned to agricultural use, though concrete ones are sometimes still used by local flying clubs. Detailed maps reveal a typical pattern of three runways, the main one usually running from SW to NE (the direction of the prevailing wind) and forming a loosely triangular shape with two subsidiary, shorter runways. Around the perimeter were dispersal points for aircraft, access roads and buildings scattered over many square miles. Hangars of various forms survive on many sites, often used for agricultural storage or light industry. The two vast hangars at Cardington, Bedfordshire are a reminder of airship days. More or less complete sets of buildings survive at several sites, including control towers, those most iconic of airfield buildings, and water towers – rural areas then had few public utilities and had to be self-sufficient in water as well as generating their own electricity. Paradoxically, the earlier airfields of the 1920s and 1930s tend to have the most surviving buildings. At Duxford and Bircham Newton we can trace the development of British air policy through representatives of every phase of building from the First World War to 1950s Cold War structures.

Above: *Watch tower and control room at RAF Watton, Norfolk*

Right: *The airfield at RAF Bentwaters, Suffolk*

History

St Edmunds Abbey in Bury was one of the richest and largest Benedictine monasteries in England. The site became home to the remains of the martyred King Edmund in 903 and the acquisition of such a notable relic made the monastery a place of pilgrimage as well as the recipient of numerous royal grants.

The Benedictine abbey itself was established in 1020. Edward the Confessor substantially enlarged the privileges in its charter and at the time of the Norman Conquest Bury ranked fourth among English abbeys in wealth and political importance. The Normans replaced the Saxon church on a grand scale using Barnack limestone. The spectacular west front was completed around the turn of the 13th century under Abbot Samson, who added a great central tower and lower octagonal towers to either side. He also improved the accommodation including a new hall, the Black Hostry, to house the abbey's many monastic visitors. In 1214 the abbey was the site of a historic meeting between King John and his dissatisfied earls and barons, as a direct result of which the *Magna Carta* was sealed at Runnymede the following year.

The abbey continued to thrive throughout the 13th century but relations with the townspeople were rarely cordial. Matters came to a head in 1327 in a summer of riots, though disputes rumbled on throughout the 14th century. The abbey suffered

Opposite: The remains of the abbot's garden wall

Below: Post-medieval houses built into the west front, with a statue of St Edmund in the foreground

other problems too, notably damage to the west tower through collapse and later a serious fire. Despite these setbacks Bury St Edmunds remained politically important throughout the 15th century – Henry VI came for Christmas in 1433 and stayed for four months – and when it was surrendered to the king in 1539 it still had a considerable income. Though the abbey precinct was quickly stripped of valuable building material, the abbot's palace survived as a house until 1720.

The abbey church: view across the crypt

Description

Visitors enter the abbey precinct today, as they have since the 14th century, through the impressive Great Gate, which originally gave access to the Great Court and the abbot's palace; the north-east corner of the abbot's garden is marked by a hexagonal tower, now a dovecote. The Great Gate is the abbey's best surviving feature and gives an excellent idea of the quality of the stonework elsewhere. The precinct wall survives well in places, and still crosses the River Lark over the Abbot's Bridge. Access to the abbey church itself was through the Norman Tower, which dates from 1120–48 (restored in Victorian times). Beyond is the once magnificent west front, into which are incorporated a range of houses built between the 16th and 18th centuries.

Enough remains of the abbey church to suggest it was an impressive structure. At over 150m long the church was one of only a few

of its date to be built on such a large scale in this country. Construction began at the semi-circular (apsidal) east end around the high altar and shrine of St Edmund. Below this and on the same plan was the crypt: the bases of its supporting piers and lower courses of its walls remain to show what a vast space this must have been, and the view from above is quite spectacular. Conspicuous among the standing remains are the piers of the crossing tower and the north wall and centre window of the north transept. The layout of some of the once extensive monastic buildings can still be seen to the north and east of the church. The chapter house, north of the north transept, contains the graves of six abbots, while the monks' cemetery and infirmary lay to the east of the church.

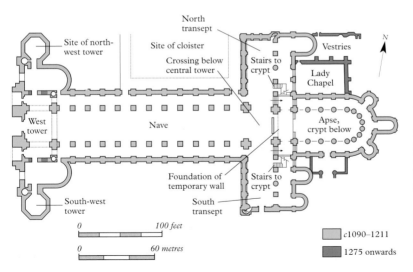

The abbey church

In the town centre, beyond Angel Hill and the Cathedral.
OS Map 155, *ref* TL 857642.
Tel 01284 764667

85

History

Leiston Abbey is one of Suffolk's most impressive monastic ruins and has some spectacular architectural features. It was founded in 1182 by Ranulf de Glanville, Henry II's Chief Justiciar, and was dedicated to St Mary. In about 1363 the abbey was moved away from what was evidently a rather unhealthy location on swampy ground, and rebuilt on its present site. The old abbey was dismantled for building materials (though a fragment of it can still be seen) and as a result the 14th-century abbey incorporates some Norman features. Robert de Ufford, Earl of Suffolk, oversaw the rebuilding of the abbey on a much larger scale than the original and included several new chapels. The outside walls were finished with fine chequerwork, while the windows had delicate Perpendicular-style tracery. The abbey was home to Augustinian canons who followed the Premonstratensian rule. Their domestic buildings were damaged by fire in the 1380s and rebuilt.

After the suppression the king bestowed the abbey on his brother-in-law Charles Brandon, Duke of Suffolk. A farmhouse was built into the corner of the nave and north transept and the abbey ruins were used as farm buildings, the church itself being used as a barn. A new front was added to the house in the Georgian period and it is currently owned by music school Pro Corda. The Lady Chapel was also restored and furnished in 1918.

View of the abbey from the south; the 16th-century porch is to the right

Description

Lying in peaceful open fields these striking ruins represent parts of the abbey church and the fairly extensive remains of the buildings around the cloister. You can enter the site through the gatehouse with its octagonal brick turret, which was built in the 16th century and leads through the west range to the cloister. As you pass through the porch the cellarer's range – used for storage – is to your left. Once in the cloister, the south range is to your right, with traces of the canon's wash-place or lavatory against the wall. At the east end of this south range are the remains of the day stairs that led up to the refectory or frater. The modern steps in their place afford a good view across the unusually well-preserved remains of the refectory and its basement, or undercroft, which has an outstanding pointed window. In the east range are the remains of the warming house (over which was the dormitory or dorter), the chapter house and the sacristy, where books and vestments were kept.

Reconstruction of the abbey as it would have looked in the 16th century

The remains of the abbey church lie to the north of the cloister: a small arch in the sacristy leads into the south transept and the magnificent north transept arch is ahead. This part of the church – the presbytery, crossing and transepts – gives you the best idea of its original stature. The crossing tower remains to a considerable height and the north transept window – one of several that survive – is around 14m high. Between the presbytery and the north transept is the Lady Chapel, now thatched and with a wooden doorway.

N of Leiston
off B1069.
OS Map 156,
ref TM 445642

*13th-century
St James's Chapel,
Lindsey*

History

There is no documentary evidence for the foundation of the Chapel of St James the Apostle at Lindsey. The earliest parts visible today date from the 13th century, but worked stones reused in the present building suggest a previous building on the site from about the middle of the 12th century: the west wall contains several characteristically Norman fragments. The chapel was almost certainly built to serve the nearby Castle of Lindsey, the earthwork remains of which are visible some 250m to the south-east, and it was probably founded by the de Cockfield family. In 1240 Nesta de Cockfield gave the churches of Kersey and Lindsey to Kersey Priory, but reserved the right to appoint the clergy for Lindsey, all of which suggests the present chapel was well established by that time. In 1242 she imposed a special tithe on parts of Cockfield – known as the Lindsey Tithes – to sustain continual lighting in the chapel.

Lindsey Castle appears to have been abandoned before the end of the 13th century but St James's Chapel continued in use. The manor and the right to appoint the warden of the chapel eventually passed to the Sampson family who appointed wardens in 1375, 1400 and 1408. Late in the 15th or early in the 16th century the chapel was repaired, and perhaps shortened, and the existing roof replaced the previous higher one. It remained in use until the Dissolution, though in somewhat reduced circumstances. In 1547 the King's Commissioners reported that its yearly value was £5, and it was one of the numerous 'free' chapels that were dissolved the same year. The king eventually granted the chapel to Thomas Turner and thereafter it was used as a barn until 1930.

Description

This small but unusual chapel sits at the edge of the village of Lindsey. It is built of flint rubble and the earliest parts are the south wall and the north-east corner, which date from the 13th century. The south wall has two simple, single-light windows of

different heights and a doorway with a less sharply pointed interior arch. The piscina, for washing the sacred vessels, appears to be original and has an interesting design, with a cusped head and two trefoil-shaped basins: features typical of the later 13th century. The west end of the north wall and the north-west window have been rebuilt. The east wall is mostly also of 13th-century date but has been much repaired.

The present simple, single-frame thatched roof dates from its use as a barn from the 16th century: the original roof is likely to have been tiled. The west wall was probably completely rebuilt when the roof was made and its pointed doorway has an early moulded-brick surround. The filling of the gable above, with its clumsy window made up of wedge-shaped blocks from an earlier arch, and now blocked, looks like a later repair. The present buttresses are later additions; the south-east buttress is probably roughly contemporary with the roof, as is the three-light east window.

Inside the chapel, looking east

On unclassified road ¹/₂ mile E of Rose Green and 8 miles E of Sudbury.
OS Map 155, ref TL 978444

MOULTON PACKHORSE BRIDGE

This medieval bridge across the River Kennet lies on the ancient route from Bury St Edmunds to Cambridge and spans a distance of over 20m. It is perhaps not strictly a packhorse bridge since it was wide enough to take carts: it is now used only by pedestrians.

The river has shrunk in size since the bridge was built in the 15th century. While a single arch would have be suitable to span a narrow stream, if used over a wider stretch this design would have created an inconveniently steep slope at both sides. At Moulton a series of smaller arches was therefore used to carry the road on a more manageable slope. The bridge is built of flint and stone rubble, with plain parapets, and the edges of the arches are made of brick. Pointed arch shapes like these were constructed using wooden formers to support and shape them, and were not used after the 15th century.

A concrete platform has been laid down alongside the bridge over the stream, at the level of the base of the piers, to allow cars to cross. The concrete extends under the arches, giving an unusual opportunity to look at the underside of the bridge.

The 15th century bridge from the south

In Moulton off B1085, 4 miles E of Newmarket. OS Map 154, ref TL 698645

MAJOR ENGLISH HERITAGE SITES

Sixteen English Heritage sites in the east of England are staffed and most have a separate guidebook, which can be purchased at the site's gift shop or through mail order. These sites charge an admission fee, although admission is free to members of English Heritage (see inside back cover). Full details of admission charges, access and opening times for all of English Heritage's sites across the country are given in the *English Heritage Members' and Visitors' Handbook* (product code: 20000), also available through mail order. Full details of English Heritage's publications can be found in the *Publications Catalogue*.

To place an order for the *Handbook*, or for any other English Heritage publication, please contact:

English Heritage Postal Sales,
c/o Gillards, Trident Works,
Temple Cloud, Bristol BS39 5AZ

Tel: 01761 452966 Fax: 01761 453408
E-mail: ehsales@gillards.com

Please always quote the product code for the publication you are ordering.

AUDLEY END HOUSE AND GARDENS
ESSEX

Built by the first Earl of Suffolk, Lord Treasurer to James I, Audley End is one of the most significant Jacobean houses in England. It was built on the scale of a royal palace, which it became in 1668 when it was bought by Charles II. Successive owners have left their stylistic imprints and the house today is a blend of many styles. The extensive landscaped parkland is the work of Lancelot 'Capability' Brown. The third Baron Braybrooke's huge picture collection and the fourth Baron's natural history collection, are also important features.

Open 1 Apr–30 Sept, Wed–Sun and bank holidays. Please call for admission prices and opening times: 01799 522399.

1 mile W of Saffron Walden on B1383.
OS Map 154, ref TL 525382.

BERNEY ARMS WINDMILL
NORFOLK

Berney Arms is one of the best and largest remaining marsh mills in Norfolk. It was built to grind a constituent of cement, and was in use until 1951, ending its days pumping water to drain surrounding marshes.

Open 1 Apr–31 Oct. Please call for admission prices

and opening times: 01493 700605.

3¹/₂ miles NE of Reedham on the N Bank of River Yare. Accessible by hire boat or by footpath from Halvergate (3¹/₂ miles)
OS Map 134, ref TG 465049.

BUSHMEAD PRIORY
BEDFORDSHIRE

Bushmead Priory was established *c* 1195 and remained a small foundation whose canons came from local families, but little else is known of its history. The survival of this Augustinian priory's medieval refectory, with its original timber roof, wall paintings and stained glass, is quite rare.

Open Jul–Aug, Sat–Sun and bank holidays. Please call for admission prices and opening times: 01234 376614.

Off B660, 2 miles S of Bolnhurst.
OS Map 153, ref TL 116607

CASTLE ACRE PRIORY
NORFOLK

Castle Acre Priory lies a short distance to the south-west of the castle and village of the same name. The priory's ruins span seven centuries and include a 12th-century church with an elaborately decorated west front which still rises to its full height, a 15th-century gatehouse and prior's lodging still fit to live in. The recreated herb garden grows both culinary and medicinal herbs.

Open year-round. Please call for admission prices and opening times: 01760 755394.

¼ mile W of village of Castle Acre, 5 miles N of Swaffham.
OS Map 132, ref TF 814148.

CASTLE RISING CASTLE
NORFOLK

A fine 12th-century domestic keep, set amid huge defensive earthworks, Castle Rising was once the palace and home to Isabella, the 'She Wolf' of France, dowager Queen of England. The keep walls stand to their original height.

Owned and managed by Mr Greville Howard. Please call for admission prices and opening times: 01553 631330.

4 miles NE of King's Lynn off A149.
OS Map 132, ref TF 666246.

DENNY ABBEY AND THE FARMLAND MUSEUM

CAMBRIDGESHIRE

Denny Abbey was founded in 1159 by Benedictine monks as a dependent priory of the great cathedral monastery of Ely. At its heart stands the medieval Franciscan refectory and the church. The Farmland Museum explores farming and village life in Cambridgeshire through the ages.

Open 1 Apr–31 Oct, noon–5pm daily. Please call for admission prices: 01223 860489. The Museum is managed by The Farmland Museum Trust.

6 miles N of Cambridge on A10.
OS Map 154, ref TL 492684.

FRAMLINGHAM CASTLE

SUFFOLK

A fine example of a late 12th-century castle, Framlingham's towers and high curtain wall are surrounded by outer defences and a picturesque mere. Recent archaeological survey has highlighted the castle's colourful history: through the ages it has served as a great baronial fortress, a prison, a poorhouse and a school.

Open year-round. Please call for admission prices and opening times: 01728 724189.

In Framlingham on B1116.
OS Map 156, ref TM 287637.

GRIME'S GRAVES
NORFOLK

Named Grim's Graves by the Anglo-Saxons after the pagan god Grim, it was not until some of them were first excavated in 1870 that they were found to be flint mines dug some 4,000 years ago. The mines provided the materials needed to make tools and weapons. Today visitors can descend 10 m by ladder into one excavated shaft. Flint-knapping demonstrations are held throughout the year.

Open year-round. Please call for admission prices and opening times: 01842 810656.

7 miles NW of Thetford off A134.
OS Map 144, ref TL 817899.

HILL HALL
ESSEX

This fine Elizabethan mansion features some of the earliest external Renaissance architectural detail in the country and rare period wall paintings of mythical and biblical subjects. Hill Hall has now been divided into private houses, but parts remain open to the public.

Open 1 Apr–30 Sep on pre-booked tours available Weds only. To book, and for admission prices, please call: 01223 582700.

M11 to jct 7 and S through Epping to Hill Hall.
OS Map 167, ref TQ 489995.

LANDGUARD FORT
SUFFOLK

Originally built during the 16th century, the remains of this fort date back to the 18th century and feature alterations made during the last hundred years. It overlooks the Orwell Estuary.

Open 6 Apr–2 Nov daily. Managed by Landguard Fort Trust. Please call for details of admission prices and opening times: 01394 277767 or 01473 218245.

1 mile S of Felixstowe: follow brown signs to Landguard Point and Nature Reserve from A414. *OS Map 169, ref TM 284319.*

LONGTHORPE TOWER
CAMBRIDGESHIRE

The tower has the finest 14th-century domestic wall paintings of secular and spiritual subjects in northern Europe, including depictions of the Wheel of Life, the Nativity and King David.

Open 1 Apr–31 Oct, Sat–Sun and bank holidays. Please call for admission prices and opening times: 01733 268482.

2 miles W of Peter-borough on A47. *OS Map 142, ref TL 162984.*

ORFORD CASTLE
SUFFOLK

Originally a keep-and-bailey castle with a walled enclosure and a great tower, Henry II constructed the building we see today as a coastal defence during the 12th century. The building records are the earliest in the kingdom. The unique polygonal keep survives almost intact with three immense towers.

Open year-round. Please call for admission prices and opening times: 01394 450472.

In Orford on B1084, 20 miles NE of Ipswich.
OS Map 169, ref TM 419499.

ROW III / OLD MERCHANT'S HOUSE / GREYFRIARS' CLOISTERS
NORFOLK

Row 111 house in Great Yarmouth, and the Old Merchant's House, which boasts fine plasterwork ceilings and oak panelling, are examples of row houses, first developed in the 13th century and unique to Great Yarmouth. Nearby are the remains of a 13th-century Franciscan friary.

Open 1 Apr–31 Oct daily by escorted tours only. Please call for admission price and tour details: 01493 857900.

In Great Yarmouth follow signs for historic quay.
OS Map 134, ref TG 525072 (houses);
TG 524073 (cloisters).

SAXTEAD GREEN POST MILL
SUFFOLK

This corn mill, the whole body of which revolves on its base, was one of many that were built in Suffolk from the late 13th century. Milling ceased in 1947 but the mill is still in working order. Climb the wooden stairs to the various floors, which are full of fascinating mill machinery.

Open 1 Apr–31 Oct. Please call for admission prices and opening times: 01728 685789.

2½ miles NW of Framlingham on A1120.
OS Map 156, ref TM 253644.

TILBURY FORT
ESSEX

The finest surviving example of 17th-century military engineering in England, Tilbury Fort was designed by Charles II's chief engineer to withstand bombardment from artillery. Today, exhibitions, the powder magazine and bunker-like 'casemates' demonstrate how the fort protected the city and you can even fire an anti-aircraft gun.

Open year-round. Please call for admission prices and opening times: 01375 858489.

½ mile E of Tilbury off A126.
OS Map 177, ref TQ 651753.

WREST PARK GARDENS
BEDFORDSHIRE

These historic gardens were laid out in the early 18th century by the de Grey family, and are a rare survivor of the formal garden style so common in 1700s England. The gardens have survived the fate of so many of their kind, that were swept away in the mid-18th century in favour of Lancelot 'Capability' Brown's natural landscape styling. Unlike Brown's landscapes Wrest relies on revelation and mystery, providing the visitor with surprises at every turn. Its grandest glory is a domed Baroque pleasure pavilion where the de Greys entertained numerous guests, kept warm by a secret heating system.

Open 1 Apr–28 Oct, Sat–Sun and bank holidays. Please call for admission prices and opening times: 01525 860152.

¾ mile E of Silsoe off A6, 10 miles S of Bedford. *OS Map 153, ref TL 091355.*

INDEX

INDEX

BEDFORDSHIRE

De Grey Mausoleum

Neale, J "Very Privately Buried": monuments in the de Grey mausoleum'. *Collections Review*, vol 4, 2003. London: English Heritage, pp 75–80

Houghton House

Collett-White, J *Inventories of Bedfordshire Country Houses 1714–1830*. Bedford: Bedfordshire Historical Record Society, vol 74, 1995, pp 103–22

Harris, J, Orgel, S and Strong, R *The King's Arcadia: Inigo Jones and the Stuart Court*. London: Arts Council of Great Britain, 1973, 109-11

CAMBRIDGESHIRESHIRE

Duxford Chapel

Orme, N and Webster, M *The English hospital 1075–1570*. New Haven/London: Yale University Press, 1995

Isleham Priory Church

A short history of the parish church of St Andrew, Isleham and the priory church of St Margaret. Ramsgate: Graham Cumming, 1961

ESSEX

Hadleigh Castle

Drewett, P L 'Excavations at Hadleigh Castle, Essex, 1971–2'. *Journal of the British Archaeological Association*, ser 3, vol 38, 1975, pp 90–154

Lexden Earthworks and Bluebottle Grove

Hunter, J *The Essex Landscape: a study of its form and history*. Chelmsford: Essex Records Office, 1999, pp 51–4

Mistley Towers

Bolton, A T *The architecture of Robert and James Adam 1758–1794*. Woodbridge: Antique Collectors' Club, 1985

Prior's Hall Barn

Sherlock, D *Prior's Hall Barn, Widdington, Essex.* London: English Heritage, 1991

St Botolph's Priory

Crossan, C, Crummy, N and Harris, A 'St Botolph's Priory'. *The Colchester Archaeologist*, vol 5, 1991–2 (1992), pp 6–10

English Heritage, *St Botolph's Priory: Colchester, Essex*. London: English Heritage, 1977

St John's Abbey Gate

Round, J H *The early charters of St John's Abbey, Colchester*. 1901

Waltham Abbey Gatehouse and Bridge

Huggins, P J 'Excavations of the Collegiate and Augustinian churches, Waltham Abbey, Essex, 1984–87'. *Archaeological Journal*, vol 146, 1989 (1991), pp 476–537

HERTFORDSHIRE

Berkhamsted Castle

Remfry, P M *Berkhamsted Castle, 1066–1495*. Malvern Link: SCS Publishing, 1995

Old Gorhambury House

Hill, N 'Conservation and Decay: two centuries at Old Gorhambury'. *Transactions of the Association for Studies in the Conservation of Historic Buildings*, vol 21, 1996, pp 36–48

RCHME *Hertfordshire Houses. Selective Inventory*. London: RCHME, 1993, pp 157–9

Roman Wall, St Albans

Niblett, R *Verulamium: the Roman city of St Albans*. Stroud: Tempus, 2001

NORFOLK

Baconsthorpe Castle

Dallas, C and Sherlock, D *Baconsthorpe Castle, excavations and finds, 1951–1972*. East Anglian

Archaeology Reports 102, 2002. Dereham: Norfolk Museums and Archaeology Service (NMAS)

Rigold, S E *Baconsthorpe Castle, Norfolk*. London: HMSO, 1966 (1981 reprint)

Binham Priory and Binham Cross

Binham Priory: a guide to the priory church of St Mary and the Holy Cross, Binham, Norfolk. Binham: Parochial Church Council, 1991

Burgh Castle and Caister Roman Fort

Gurney, D 'The Saxon Shore in Norfolk' in Margeson, A, Ayers, B and Heywood, S (eds) *A festival of Norfolk archaeology*. Norwich: Norfolk and Norwich Archaeological Society, 1996, pp 30–9

— *Outposts of the Roman Empire: a guide to Norfolk's Roman forts at Burgh Castle, Caister-on-Sea and Brancaster*. Norwich: Norfolk Archaeological Trust, 2002

Castle Acre Castle and Bailey Gate

Coad, J G and Streeten, A D F 'Excavations at Castle Acre Castle, Norfolk, 1972–77: country house and castle of the Norman earls of Surrey'. *Archaeological Journal*, vol 139, 1982, pp 138–301

English Heritage *Castle Acre Castle and Priory* London: English Heritage, 1998

Church of the Holy Sepulchre

Hare, J N 'The Priory of the Holy Sepulchre, Thetford'. *Norfolk Archaeology*, vol 37, 1979, pp 190–200

Cow Tower, Norwich

Ayers, B S, Smith, R and Tillyard, M 'The Cow Tower, Norwich: a detailed survey and partial reinterpretation'. *Medieval Archaeology*, vol 32, 1988, pp 184–207

Creake Abbey

Bedingfeld, A L and Gilyard-Beer, R *Creake Abbey, Norfolk*. London: HMSO, 1970

North Elmham Chapel

Heywood, S *The site of the Anglo-Saxon Cathedral and the Bishops Chapel at North Elmham*. North Elmham Parish Council, 1998

Rigold, S E *North Elmham Saxon Cathedral, Norfolk*. London: English Heritage, 1985

St Olave's Priory

Davis, K R *St Olave's Priory, Herringfleet, Suffolk*. London: HMSO, 1975

Thetford Priory and Thetford Warren Lodge

Raby, F J E, Baillie Reynolds, P K and Rigold, S E *Thetford Priory, Norfolk*. London: HMSO, 1979

Wilcox, R 'Thetford Cluniac priory excavations 1971–4'. *Norfolk Archaeology*, vol 40, 1987, pp 1–18

Weeting Castle

McGee, C and Perkins, J *Analytical archive report on Weeting Castle*. London: English Heritage, 1995

SUFFOLK

Bury St Edmunds Abbey

Gransden, A (ed) *Bury St Edmunds: medieval art, architecture, archaeology and economy*. British Archaeological Association Conference Transactions XX, 1998

Whittingham, A B *Bury St Edmunds Abbey, Suffolk*. London: English Heritage, 1992

Leiston Abbey

DoE *Leiston Abbey, Suffolk*. London: HMSO, 1971

Lindsey/St James's Chapel

Bridge, M *Tree-ring analysis of timbers from the Chapel of St James, Kersey Road, Rose Green, Lindsey, Suffolk*. Portsmouth: English Heritage CfA, 2002

Moulton Packhorse Bridge

Cook, M *Medieval bridges*. Shire Archaeology 77. Princes Risborough: Shire, 1998

FEATURES

Bulwarks Against Invasion

French, P W *Coastal Defences: processes, problems and solutions*. London: Routledge, 2001

Kent, P *Fortifications of East Anglia*. Lavenham: Terence Dalton, 1988

Priors, Pilgrims and Prelates

Coppack, G *Abbeys and priories*. London: English Heritage, 1990

Wilton, J W *Monastic life in Norfolk and Suffolk*. Fakenham: Acorn Editions, 1980

Harnessing the Wind

Apling, H *Norfolk corn windmills*. Norwich: Norfolk Windmills Trust, 1984

Howes, H *Bedfordshire mills*. Bedford: Bedfordshire County Council, 1983

Woodward-Nutt, J *Mills open: windmills and watermills open to the public*. London: Society for the Protection of Ancient Buildings, 2000

Creative Angles

Belsey, H *Thomas Gainsborough: a country life*. London/Munich: Prestel, 2002

Brown, D B, Hemingway, A and Lyles, A *Romantic Landscape: the Norwich school of painters*. London: Tate Gallery Publishing, 2000

Peacock, C *John Constable: the man and his work*. London: John Baker, 1971

An Unsinkable Battleship

Bowman, M W *Fields of Little America*. Peterborough: GMS Enterprises, 2001

Bowyer, Michael J F *Action Stations. Wartime military airfields of East Anglia, 1939–1945*. Wellingborough: Patrick Stephens, 1990

Useful websites relating to the east of England

www.english-heritage.org.uk
(English Heritage)

www.museums.bedfordshire.gov.uk/localgroups/bac.html
(Bedfordshire archaeological groups)

www.broads-authority.gov.uk
(The Broads Authority)

www.cambridge.gov.uk
(Cambridge City Council)

www.camcnty.gov.uk
(Cambridgeshire County Council)

www.eastofenglandtouristboard.com
(East of England Tourist Board)

www.essexcc.gov.uk
(Essex County Council)

www.hertsdirect.org/heritage/archaeology
(Hertfordshire archaeological information)

www.nationaltrust.org.uk
(National Trust)

www.norwich.gov.uk
(Norwich City Council)

www.norfolkwindmills.co.uk
(Norfolk Windmills Trust)

www.norfolk.gov.uk/tourism/museums
(Norfolk Museums and Archaeology Service)

www.suffolkarch.org.uk
(Suffolk Institute of Archaeology and History)

www.smg.uk.com
(Suffolk Mills Group)